MURDER GOES SOLO

A PIPER HAYDN PIANO MYSTERY BOOK ONE

MALISSA CHAPIN

IVORY KEYS PRESS LLC

Published by **Ivory Keys Press LLC 2022 Oshkosh, Wisconsin PO Box 1796 Oshkosh, WI 54903**

Scripture: King James Version

Cover Design by: BeckandDot Covers

Editing by: Jonathan Wright

CONTENTS

To all my piano teachers:
Mrs. Kamakian—Racine, Wisconsin
Mrs. Paula Cole—Appleton, Wisconsin
Dr. Jon Ensminger—Dunbar, Wisconsin
And my first one,
Mrs. Jean Hurd—New Virginia, Iowa
Thank you!

Music is the space between the notes.

—Claude Debussy

None of this would have happened if the Steinway had been delivered on time.

CHAPTER ONE

Tuesday

P iper blew out a breath and clenched her teeth as she marched down the hall of the Haydn Music Academy toward her office. She planned to call Notes Music Centre and give them a piece of her frazzled mind. The recital was scheduled for this evening, and the Steinway she'd ordered a year ago waited at the warehouse—not on her stage.

Piano music floated into the hall from a practice room, and Piper peeked around the door. "I love the sound of your piece, Grace. But when you play that phrase, pay attention to the crescendo."

Grace nodded and returned to her practice. The careful playing resumed, and Piper smiled at the crisp crescendo. "That's my girl," she whispered.

Piper breezed into her office and dropped into her chair with a groan. The Haydn Music Academy's senior piano recital lacked a piano. She whispered, "I should know no one in Cranberry Harbor moves at a normal pace." Piper Haydn loved her hometown. The charming central Wisconsin town boasted quaint shops and a clean, family-friendly beach—a respite from the busy pace of modern-day city life. But today the slow pace of Cranberry Harbor gave her a twitching eye.

The phone rang. "Haydn Music Academy. Piper speaking."

"Piper, Trefor Vaughn here."

She took a deep breath before answering the man. She wanted to speak pleasant words to her friend, but her patience was long gone, and her nerves crackled with stress. A headache formed behind her eyes, and her self-control slipped away. "Trefor, where is my Steinway?" she snapped.

"Whoa, Piper—I'm sorry. But we loaded your piano onto the truck five minutes ago, and the driver backed out of the loading dock headed your way."

Piper rubbed her forehead and breathed a sigh of relief. "You told me the same thing two days ago, and you said the same thing this morning. Are you positive this time?"

"Positive . . . sorry about the mix-up. But your piano is definitely on the truck and heading your way. I'll drive over to direct the unloading, and the piano tuner will come an hour later. Don't worry. You'll be playing that beauty in no time."

"I have students arriving—again—for the uncrating, and the recital starts at seven. I hope nothing else goes wrong. You know this delivery is cutting things way too close. The Steinway hasn't settled, and I shouldn't even use it tonight."

"I know. I'm sorry for the stress. It's coming—honest."

"Thanks, Trefor. I know it's not your fault, but I wanted it here days ago to avoid this pressure right before show-time."

Trefor chuckled. The sound was a burst of deep warm laughter that soothed her frazzled nerves. "I've never known you to go into a recital unstressed, Piper."

"Ouch. You know me too well. Get over here, and let's get my new baby ready to roll."

"See you in a few."

Piper hung up and glanced around her office. Recital programs were piled near the door in a messy heap. Papers, bags, and empty coffee cups trailed across every surface, and a porcelain frog rested in front of her computer. She frowned and grabbed the frog, turning it over to examine the markings. Nothing. She rubbed her temples again and dug in her Chanel bag for a pain reliever before her headache worsened.

Piper had saved money for ten years to buy a Steinway grand piano. The price tag for the beautiful instrument hurt—even for a Haydn.

Her friend Trefor had called three days ago. Her piano was on the truck and on the way to the academy. She had called her senior students, and everyone hurried to the academy to watch the uncrating and piano set up. Piper wanted to share the thrill of the new piano's arrival with her best and brightest students.

Her students had practiced their Debussy pieces for months under Piper's watchful teaching. The students polished their pieces this week—adding dynamics and emotion to meet Piper's expectations. Some parents believed she asked too much from a bunch of kids, but the success of her academy students proved that Piper's methods worked. She expected dedication and progress from her students, and in turn, they received a rigorous musical education.

The students had milled around the auditorium, talking and teasing each other while waiting for the piano's arrival. Piper answered practice questions and gave technique advice to help her students polish their pieces before the big show. She reminded students of the dress code—concert attire—and checked her watch repeatedly until the phone rang.

"There's a mix-up, Piper. No piano today," Trefor had said.

This morning was unfolding in an almost identical repeat. The kids groaned, and Piper attempted to show patience, but she sent the kids home with a sigh and promised to call next time Notes Music Centre pledged to deliver.

The recital started in a few hours and the auditorium had no piano. The mess in her office didn't help her growing anger.

"Lisa, was Roosevelt in here?" Piper leaned out her office door and called to her receptionist.

"Yeah, sorry about that. I meant to pick up before you saw the aftermath." Lisa said. "I was printing the recital programs, and Rosie ran in there muttering. But I didn't hear anything she said." She smiled an "I'm sorry" sort of grin and turned back to the desk. "Want me to call her to come back and clean up?"

Piper sighed. Asking Rosie to clean up her messes was similar to asking the wind to stop blowing. She would only create a bigger mess trying to restore order. "No, but if you want to come down for the piano delivery, you're welcome to join us."

"Will Trefor be there?" Lisa asked with a grin.

"Yes, he said he's on the way to direct the uncrating."

Lisa fluffed her hair and smoothed her blouse. "You talked me into it."

Piper checked her watch. She had no time to clean her messy office before the Steinway and her students arrived. She grabbed her coffee mug and hurried to the auditorium with sparkling eyes and a pounding heart. Having a Steinway piano available for her students was a dream come true. Her students added culture to the town, and the Steinway added a layer of style and class to the academy.

After the city built a shiny new school at the edge of town, Piper purchased the old schoolhouse. The classrooms and auditorium fit her music academy perfectly, but the old building needed constant upkeep. She kept the old chalkboards and the sign over the door but updated most of the building. A huge loan from her father and the elbow grease of friends and family allowed Piper to open her music academy doors five years ago. The Haydn Music Academy employed forty teachers and cranked out prize-winning pianists, vocalists, and dancers, surpassing her wildest dreams. Her students ranged from babies to adults studying various instruments, choir music, dance, and art. Piper adored her dream-come-true academy—but she would lose her cool if that piano wasn't delivered today.

--Be there in 5.

--Thanks, Trefor. Hope it's for sure this time.

--Ha. Yes. I promise.

Piper hurried down the hall, thankful for her mug's spill-proof lid, and entered Rosie's number.

"Hey."

"Hey yourself, Roosevelt. Where are you? The Steinway is on the truck."

Rosie laughed. "Waiting for this piano is worse than waiting for a baby. Are you sure this time?"

"I hope so. Come on down."

"I'm on my way, and don't call me Roosevelt."

Piper chuckled and hung up. Rosie and her four siblings sported presidential names—Kennedy, Lincoln, Harrison, and Truman. Piper teased Rosie all the time about her historical moniker, but Rosie was her cherished friend.

Piper smiled as she passed classrooms. Students worked on pieces or listened to the term's composer—Debussy. She waved to the janitor at the end of the hall. "Hey—the piano is on the way. Can you vacuum the stage and polish the piano before our recital?"

He nodded. "Sure thing, Piper."

"Thanks, Don." She hurried to the parking lot as Trefor and the vehicles from Notes Music Centre pulled into the academy parking lot.

"Trefor!" Piper called as her tall friend unfolded from his pale blue Prius.

He smiled and waved, grabbing his Yeti tumbler and gulping. He wore a bright red cardigan and a music print shirt. Colorful socks peeked out from under his skinny jeans. Trefor stopped to gather his wavy brown hair into a man bun and adjust his shades. "Your big day," he said and rested his arm around Piper's shoulder.

Piper stepped away from his hug and turned to the students gathered behind her. She smiled at her chattering kids and the beautiful cloudless sky. The delivery truck beeped while backing into the loading dock, and a crowd gathered on the sidewalk. Trefor called greetings to several students. Everyone knew everyone else in Cranberry Harbor, and Trefor was a town favorite. He worked at the music store, teaching lessons and selling pianos. Piper had heard he even substituted at the public school, helping with the choirs.

"Nice socks," she said and laughed.

Trefor wiggled his eyebrows and pulled up one leg of his skinny jeans. "Music notes."

Lisa ran up behind them, breathless from jogging to the back door. "Rosie's on her way. Oh, hi, Trefor," she said, a smile plastered on her face and her eyelashes fluttering.

Trefor nodded and gave a small wave.

Piper's eyes sparkled, and she resisted the urge to jump up and down and clap her hands like a little girl. Waiting for the Steinway reminded her of Christmas morning. The extreme time crunch before the recital tonight the only damper on her excitement.

"Is your dad coming for the uncrating, Piper?" Trefor asked as he waved the truck driver back to the sidewalk.

"If you delivered the piano when you promised, he would have been here." She teased and punched his arm.

Trefor frowned and rubbed his arm. "Ow. I'm sorry—again."

"At least I didn't have to reschedule the recital. But to answer your question, no. Dad is meeting with a big corporation to sell our chocolate cherries."

"Trefor—glad you could make it!" Rosie called with her bracelets clanking as she ran toward them. "Is the Steinway *actually* here this time?"

"Yes, Rosie, it's on that very truck as we speak," Trefor said, his voice clipped.

Rosie clapped her hands and kissed Piper on the cheek. "How exciting, Piper! Who gets to tickle the ivories first?"

"I'd say me, but the time . . . and I have to change. And ahem," Piper cleared her throat. "My office is a mess." She frowned.

Rosie smiled. "Sorry. I told Lisa I'd come back to clean."

Lisa stepped toward Trefor, grabbing his arm and leaning into his side.

Trefor pulled his arm away and buttoned his cardigan. He readjusted his man bun and stepped away from Lisa. "Excuse me." He walked over to the truck and talked to the driver, gesturing and pointing.

"What's all that about?" Rosie asked, frowning.

"I don't know. I wish they'd hurry." Piper adjusted the floral scarf at her neck, tying it in a loose knot. She clapped her hands and squealed. "I can't wait!"

Rosie smiled and gave her a quick hug.

The janitor opened the backstage doors, and the driver reversed the truck into the opening. A man jumped out and pulled the cargo doors open. He locked a ramp into place and disappeared into the back of the truck.

Trefor ran over to Piper, his feet sliding in his Birkenstocks on the gravel driveway.

"Piper, can you and the students gather inside? You'll have a better view when they roll your Steinway onto the stage."

Piper frowned. "I planned to oversee the entire delivery process, Trefor. You know I've waited so long for this day."

"Trust me," he said. "Get everyone in the hall, and I'll make sure your new baby stays safe and sound. We'll open the crate and let the piano tuner get to work. Your recital will start on time. I promise." Trefor stepped close and leaned down, but Piper stepped away and frowned. Piper was skittish around men and didn't plan to date for a long time. When Daniel Graves left her at the altar, she swore off men for good. She didn't want to hurt Trefor's feelings, but he wasn't her type—not with those skinny jeans and man bun. She shuddered.

"Students, they asked us to move to the hall." She and Rosie corralled the students into the auditorium. "Fill the front row, please," she instructed, then paced. "Let's move in and get out of their way."

"Why are you nervous?" Rosie asked, settling in the seat next to Piper's students. She tucked her flowy skirt under her legs and stuck out her tongue at one of the boys, and he giggled. "Trefor was getting a bit close out there, Piper. What's up with that?"

Piper rolled her eyes. "I don't know, but he knows I'm not interested." She pointed to the eavesdropping students and whispered, "Shh."

The doors opened, and Trefor and two men pushed a massive wooden crate onto the stage. Don followed close behind, picking up leaves from the carpet.

"Where do you want the piano, Piper?" Trefor asked, standing mid-stage, his hands on his hips. He glanced around the stage and walked to the middle. "Here?"

Piper joined him and pointed to the spot she marked earlier near stage left.

Trefor shook his head. "No, the piano belongs in the middle." He pointed the delivery men to the middle of the stage.

"Excuse me, gentlemen, but I chose this spot." Piper frowned and glanced at the crate.

Trefor waved her away. "We'll uncrate the piano over here so the students can watch. When my technicians attach the pedals and legs, we will position the Steinway anywhere you wish." He smiled and turned back to the stage.

Rosie jumped from her seat. "What's he doing? It's *your* piano. Your *stage*, I might add."

"I don't know. The men must need more space to open the crate and assemble the piano."

Rosie patted Piper's back. "Well, I don't appreciate him disrespecting you in front of your students."

"Thanks, Rosie."

The two women waited at the side of the stage while the deliverymen eased the crate off the piano dollies. Trefor barked orders at the men and directed their movements.

"I guess he knows what he's doing. He does this for a living." Piper said.

When Rosie ran her fingers through her curls, her earrings clanked. "Well, Miss Music Academy Owner, he may sell pianos, but you're the one who plunked down eighty thousand dollars to buy a Steinway. He should not boss you around."

Piper smiled. "Don't remind me of the cost. Ugh. I could have repaired half my house with that money."

Rosie sniffed. "Money well spent. The Steinway gives the academy an air of respectability and pizzazz."

Piper laughed. "Rosie, you give us all the pizzazz we need." The women stepped near center stage while the men pried the crate open. Piper caught a glimpse of the shiny black wood, and her heart squeezed. She had dreamed of owning a Steinway for decades, and her dream was about to come true. Smiling at Rosie, she rested her hand on her heart and glanced around. Her students smiled, and excitement bubbled into loud voices and restless shifting. Lisa snapped photos, and Piper nodded, flashing her a thumbs up.

When Piper turned back to the stage, her heart pounded, and her hands trembled. Hard work and years of careful saving fulfilled her dream of owning a Steinway. Mission accomplished.

The men pried at the sides of the crate. The wood splintered in a loud crack, and the men jumped back as the sides of the container thudded to the floor.

Later Piper would say that everything happened in slow motion. The splintering crate, the flash of shiny black wood, the exploding screams, and rolling nausea. But in real life, everything happened at once.

A student screamed, "Is that a hand?"

The world stopped—the hall silent. Piper treaded through deep water in slow motion. She moved to the crate as the pale-faced men backed away. Her stomach lurched as screaming erupted around the hall. Noises faded into the background. She trudged through a tunnel. Underneath the open lid of her long-awaited Steinway lay Daniel Graves, the man who had jilted her at the altar.

The auditorium exploded into a cacophony of sounds. Piper shouted, "Rosie, get the students out of here!" She whirled back to the stage. The delivery men stood at the edge of the piano crate gasping for breath, their faces pale.

"Step away! Call the police!" Piper yelled, and her stomach lurched. She jumped back from the crate.

Trefor sank onto the stage steps and rested his head in his hands. Screams echoed around the auditorium. Pale-faced people stood rooted in their spots staring at the stage—unable to look away or move.

Piper sat next to Trefor, choking back sobs.

"What's happening to this world?" Trefor asked, his eyes wet with tears. Trefor rested his arm on Piper's shoulders and pulled her close to his side. She took deep breaths as her mind churned.

"I don't know, Trefor. It's sick. My poor students." She shivered.

Trefor pulled her close and rubbed her arms. "Are you cold, Piper? Do you need a jacket?"

"I don't know. I can't think straight right now." She blew out a breath and tried to calm her churning stomach. She rested her head on Trefor's shoulder, unable to sit up straight and unwilling to look at the piano crate.

"What was it? What did you see?" he asked.

Piper sat frozen, unable to form the words. Her mind was mush, and her tongue thick and wooly. "Daniel," she croaked through dry lips.

Trefor pulled away and stared at Piper. "Daniel? Graves? *Your* Daniel?" His voice slipped up an octave as he shot out the questions.

Piper nodded and burst into tears.

Trefor pulled her back into his arms and rested his head on hers. "I'm so sorry," he murmured over and over.

Piper let Trefor hold her. She needed to feel safe for a moment before the police came. But sitting feet away from Daniel's body did nothing to calm her spirits.

Piper glanced around the hall. Lisa sat in the back row, and her students waited in the foyer—the auditorium door closed. "Who's with the students?" she called.

"Rosie," Lisa said.

Everyone in the auditorium had stood frozen in their spots when the crate opened. Now the delivery drivers stepped away from the container and plopped onto the floor. Their faces were gray, and their eyes bugged out. One man grabbed his stomach and leaned forward, and another wiped his eyes.

Piper shuddered, and Trefor pulled her closer. His beard tickled her cheek, and he smelled of coffee and something she couldn't decipher—probably that hand sanitizer he constantly used. She stared at the floor, Trefor's bright socks in her line of vision. The colors blurred and danced in front of her eyes.

She sighed. "I'm glad you're here, Trefor. It's so awful."

He nodded his head, his beard tickling her cheek again. "I'm glad too. I need to call my boss—he needs to talk to the police too." Trefor pushed off the steps leaving her alone, shivering and afraid.

She glanced around the hall but refused to look at the stage. She had no desire to see the crate or its contents. Her stomach lurched at the memory of Daniel's blank face staring at her from inside the Steinway.

Piper's worst memory of Daniel was his retreating back running out of the church. He had left her standing at the altar in her wedding dress, staring at the church full of people.

A body in the Steinway is a thousand times worse.

Daniel's face and lifeless blue eyes staring out of her brand new Steinway flashed through Piper's mind, and she gagged. She bolted for the entrance searching for a trash can, hoping to find one in time.

Halfway down the aisle, Lisa met her with a trash can, and Piper grabbed it without a moment to spare. She wiped her mouth on the plastic bag, gasping for air as tears ran down her cheeks.

Lisa waited. "You okay, hon? I'm so sorry."

Piper nodded. "I don't think I'll ever be okay, but I'm fine for this moment. Oh, Lisa." A strangled sob bubbled in her throat, but Piper choked it back.

No time for crying.

"Did you see who was in there?" Lisa whispered.

"Daniel," Piper said and tears rolled down her cheek.

"*Your* Daniel?" Lisa's jaw dropped.

"He's not my Daniel anymore, but yes, the one and only Mr. Graves." Piper sobbed and wiped her eyes on her sleeve. "I'm a mess." She tried to straighten her pink floral scarf, but her hands trembled.

"Hey, Piper," Lisa whispered. "No one expects you to look like a magazine photo." She reached for Piper's hand and held it. "Breathe ... in ... out. ... You got it." Lisa smiled and patted her back. "You're going to survive this."

"Of all the things that could go wrong on recital day, I never imagined this." She sighed. "What a horrible day!"

"His day's not so great either." Lisa pointed to the stage.

"Lisa. That's not funny."

"No, you're right. It's not," Lisa said and bit her lip.

The wail of sirens sounded in the street. The entire Cranberry Harbor Police Department rushed through her doors.

Piper stepped toward a row of chairs, expecting officers to burst into the hall.

She frowned and stepped into the hallway. Students leaned against the wall, and two officers talked to Rosie. Other officers ran through halls opening and shutting classroom doors, and a dog sniffed the baseboards.

Piper stepped into the huddle. "I'm Piper Haydn, the owner. The body is this way."

"Body?" said the older officer. "We got a call for a bomb threat."

The students screamed and bolted for the front door. Police officers herded the children outside.

Piper dropped to the floor in the middle of the foyer and rested her head in her hands.

What is going on? Who's doing this to me? Why?

The older officer stepped over to her and bent down. "Ma'am, our officers are clearing the building, but you have to wait outside." Piper nodded, and Rosie helped her to her feet.

"What about the body?" she asked.

The officer frowned and pulled out a notebook. "Where is it?"

She pointed to the auditorium doors behind her. "In there. In the piano."

He stopped writing and closed his eyes. "Do you mean *at* the piano?"

"No. *In. In* the piano," Piper whispered.

He barked orders to the officers. "Weston and Burns, secure the hall! Dahl, bring that dog back here!" He turned to Piper. "Ma'am, go outside until the dogs clear the building but do not go anywhere. No one leaves."

Piper nodded. *How did my world change in an instant?*

Moments earlier, her music academy was preparing for a senior recital, and her life seemed perfect, everything in place—other than Rosie's mess in the office. Her goals and dreams had crumbled more quickly than she could blink—everything had fallen apart in the worst way imaginable.

What else can go wrong? What's worse than finding my ex-fiancé in my Steinway crate?

Her stomach lurched at the memory of Daniel's dead eyes.

"Come on," Rosie said. "Let's get you outside."

Students swarmed around Piper and Rosie when they stepped through the doors.

"What was that?"

"What's going on?"

"I called my mom."

"Are we still having the recital?"

Piper's head whipped around at the last question. "Who asked that? No. No recital." She sighed and pinched the bridge of her nose.

Rosie herded the students away from Piper, assuring them in hushed tones.

A crowd gathered across the street, watching the sirens and flashing lights. An officer strung crime scene tape across the driveway and motioned the group to move away.

That's good—I can't handle questions right now.

She couldn't think. Couldn't decide what to do. The whole situation was surreal and fake. For a moment, she hoped the body was a joke. Or a reality TV prank. But no, Daniel's vacant eyes were all too real.

Rosie stepped behind her and whispered, "News vans."

"No. Not good."

"And, all the moms will come for pickup soon. You better hope a police officer comes out here to talk to them. I'm not getting between kids and their mamas." Rosie grimaced.

Piper nodded. "I should ask for an officer to come out before that happens." She shuddered, anticipating the chaos when parents learned their children had to wait at the academy.

Rosie rested a hand on Piper's shoulder. "The officers told us to stay outside."

"Well, I'm not facing parents alone, Rosie." Piper marched to the academy doors, searching for backup. The officer who sent them outside stood inside the doorway. She motioned, and the man stuck his head out the door, frowning.

"What?"

"I need someone to speak to unhappy parents when they learn their children can't leave. I didn't get your name. Officer . . . ?"

"Chief Maxwell. Give me a minute. We're stretched a bit thin in here. Someone will come out as soon as possible." He shut the door in Piper's face, leaving her staring into her academy.

"Thanks a lot, Chief Maxwell," she said to the closed door and sighed. Her staff and students spread across the parking lot, huddled in small groups. She wanted to walk around the clustered students and hug each one. She wanted to assure them that everything was fine, but her gritty eyes and throbbing head held her back. She didn't

have information and didn't know what to say. She moved around
the huddled groups in a daze, crippled by shock.

I have no idea how we'll survive this.

"They didn't teach this at Juilliard," she whispered. "'What to Do
with a Body in Your Steinway 101.'" She stifled a nervous giggle
before someone could inform the police that Piper was maniacally
laughing in the parking lot.

Rosie waved her over and gave her another hug. The students
gathered around Rosie with pale faces and tired eyes.

Piper forced a tight smile. "I'm so sorry." She swallowed over the
lump in her throat. "I don't know what to say or how to fix this."

The students nodded. "I want my mom," Tom McClure said.

Piper smiled. Tom, the big, almost grown-up boy, needed his
mom. "If it makes you feel any better, Tom, I want my mom too."

"Did the officer tell you anything?" Rosie asked.

"We have to wait 'til they clear the building. No one leaves. If the
parents come before he sends an officer out, we have to hold them
off."

"Oh, boy," Rosie said. "That's gonna be fun." She whistled and
rolled her eyes.

"We can't see our moms?" Finley Wright wailed while tears rolled
down her pale cheeks.

"Not until the officers talk to us. I'm sorry." Piper said.

What a nightmare.

Her staff huddled with the students offering calm and comfort.
Piper spoke with each adult repeating the officer's instructions and
attempting to reassure students. She tried to answer questions that
had no answers.

"What's going on?" an angry voice called from the street.

"And the mothers have arrived," Rosie whispered.

Piper grimaced and walked to the police barrier, scanning for an
available officer. "Mrs. Ford. I'm so sorry. The police came because
of a threat, and we all have to wait until the officers clear us. No one
can leave."

"What?" Mrs. Ford and several other parents yelled with shrill voices.

"Piper Haydn, you give me my children right now! Right now!"

Piper turned to see her least favorite parent marching up to the crime tape. Mrs. Schmidt always found a reason to complain. A teacher's look. The fee structure. The temperature in the studio. The tuning on the pianos. Piper knew the fur would fly in approximately two seconds if she didn't think fast.

"I'm sorry, Mrs. Schmidt. I . . ."

"No one leaves, ma'am. That's not Miss Haydn's doing. That's mine." Chief Maxwell reached out and shook the mother's hand. "Now if the parents will step back, we'll talk to your children as soon as we terminate the bomb threat."

"Bomb?"

"What?"

"What's going on?"

The crowd erupted into loud questions, and a microphone appeared out of nowhere.

"Sir, did you say *bomb?*" a reporter asked.

He held up his hand. "No comment. Everyone back up. Now. And leave Miss Haydn and her teachers alone. They're keeping your children safe until I release them."

He turned and marched back to the building, leaving Piper to hold off the angry parents.

She remembered the book her mom read when she was small—*Alexander and the Terrible, Horrible, No Good, Very Bad Day*. "If this isn't an Alexander day, I don't know what is," she whispered.

Piper scanned the crowd of students and staff huddled around the parking lot and lawn. Everything she had sacrificed for was imploding, and she was powerless to stop the destruction. She blocked out the yells from upset parents but wished she could march to the police tape and answer their questions. She knew the parents didn't understand, but the chief took that decision out of her hands. She wasn't in charge of her academy right now.

Trefor stood in the middle of the parking lot, rubbing his eyes and bending over, gasping for air.

"Are you all right, Trefor?"

"It's so surreal. Man . . . I just . . ." He blew out a breath and rubbed his beard. His hair fell out of the man bun and hung around his shoulders.

Piper glanced out to Glacier Lake and the blue sky and fluffy white clouds. She frowned. "It doesn't seem possible to have such a beautiful sunshiny day out here and so much ugliness in there."

"Yeah, the dissonance," Trefor said. He wrapped his arms around Piper, and she allowed the intrusion into her space.

She rested her head on his shoulder for a moment before pushing away. "How do I fix this? So awful." She rubbed her eyes and blew out a breath.

"We're in this together. You got that? I'm here for you, Piper."

She nodded, relief flooding her heart. Yes, they were in this together. Trefor understood her shock. The vision of Daniel in the piano kept flashing through her mind—her stomach twisted. She closed her eyes and took a deep breath. "I love this town, Trefor. A murder is devastating to everyone. We don't worry about things this twisted in Cranberry Harbor. It's not that kind of town."

He nodded. "It's sick."

"Piper." Ruby stood outside the crime tape waving. "I brought hot coffee and white chocolate chip cookies," Ruby called, pointing to her cart.

Tears stung the back of Piper's eyes as she hurried over. "Oh, Ruby—thank you."

Ruby reached to hug Piper and whispered, "Be strong. You've got this, and we're here for you." She pushed the cart under the tape to Piper and waved as she retreated.

Piper sighed. She hoped the officers would solve this problem and return Cranberry Harbor to the safe, charming town they all adored. Ruby's kindness was the Cranberry Harbor she knew—caring for each other by offering food, smiles, and hugs.

Piper pushed Ruby's coffee cart to a clustered group and passed out steaming hot coffee and fresh-from-the-oven cookies.

"Who brought these?" Rosie asked.

"Ruby."

"Oh. I love Ruby's coffee. She's so sweet." Rosie's bracelets clanked as she waved her arms. "I can't believe this, Piper. Who would do this?"

"I don't know," Piper said with a sigh. "I hurt for the students who saw the scene. No one should ever see what we saw in that auditorium today."

Rosie nodded. Her dangling earrings swung and clanked, ringing like a tiny bell. "It's gonna work out, Piper. Keep the faith."

A strangled laugh escaped from Piper's throat. "Faith? Right now I have more *questions* for God than faith."

"Me too, Piper, but hold on. The police will fix this in time. They have to."

"I'm so glad they didn't deliver the piano earlier in the day. Every class is full in the early hours, and all the little ones . . ." Piper's voice trailed off.

Trefor grabbed a cup of coffee. "I'm glad too, Piper. Poor kids. Poor *us.*" He shivered and gulped his coffee.

"Trefor? What do you think? Is it possible that Daniel was in that piano since your first scheduled delivery?" Rosie whispered.

Trefor blanched, and Piper grimaced. "No, Rosie. I won't believe that," Trefor said. "Working for days with that poor man in the crate right in our storage area? No, not possible." Trefor crushed his coffee cup, and dribbles of coffee ran down his arm. Rosie grabbed a napkin and patted the coffee off his sweater.

"Don't worry, Trefor. We're all upset—awful," she said.

"Everyone okay over here?" Lisa asked, reaching for a cup of coffee.

"Well, okay as we can be in this situation," Piper said. "How about you?"

Lisa sighed. "I'm not sure. I want this awful mess gone."

"Well, that's four of us, Lisa," Rosie said, pointing around the circle.

Piper passed out coffee and focused on her teachers and students who came to grab a treat. Her mind wandered, and she couldn't form words.

I'm saying the same thing over and over. How am I going to survive this, Lord? Any ideas?

She remembered a favorite Bible verse: "Cast all your care on him, for he cares for you."

I'm casting, Lord. Help.

"Miss Haydn." An officer motioned her to the door. "Chief Maxwell wants to see you now."

Piper followed the officer inside and groaned at her disheveled academy.

They're doing their job.

"Piper." Chief Maxwell stepped from a cluster of officers. "Can we talk in your office?"

She nodded and led the police chief down the hall. She pushed Rosie's mess aside, grabbing files from a chair. She wiped a shaky hand across her clammy forehead.

Chief Maxwell sat on the other side of her desk and pulled out his notebook. "Why don't you tell me what happened here today?" He stared across the desk.

A chill ran up Piper's spine.

He wants me to confess to storing Daniel in the Steinway.

"Well, Chief Maxwell, I have a recital scheduled for this evening. On Friday, Notes Music Centre promised to deliver my new Steinway piano. They had called and delayed the delivery several times until they finally delivered my piano this afternoon—with a body inside. That's all I can tell you."

He frowned. "Who called in the bomb threat?"

"I have no idea. I didn't know about a bomb threat until you shooed us outside."

"*Removed to safety,* Miss Haydn. Not shooed."

"Sorry." She bit back a sarcastic reply and tapped her foot on the floor. This man's attitude wasn't endearing.

"Let's go back to the first date you expected your piano. . . . What did you call it?"

"A Steinway."

"What's that?"

Piper rolled her eyes and took a deep breath. She plastered on her polite, professional smile. "Steinway is a premier brand of piano handcrafted at the Steinway factory in New York City. They build pianos from maple and mahogany with a diaphragmatic soundboard—"

The chief held up his hand. "I don't need all that information. Steinway is the brand?"

"Yes, the brand."

"How much did this piano cost, and where did you purchase it?"

"I ordered it from Notes Music Centre downtown, and I paid eighty thousand dollars plus tax."

Chief Maxwell coughed and his eyes bugged out. He turned his head and cleared his throat. "Excuse me?"

"What?"

"*How much?* You paid eighty thousand bucks for the piano in that crate?"

"Yes, is that a problem?" She narrowed her eyes and bit back a stinging reply. She had saved money for years for her dream Steinway—now nightmare. She didn't need to justify her life goals to this clueless man. He apparently lacked class—fine instruments beyond his understanding.

"There is no problem. I didn't realize anyone spent that kind of money on a piano." He raised his eyebrows.

Piper raised her chin and took a deep breath. "Shall we continue? My students want to go home."

"My officers will work on that. They will release your students while we talk. Back to the piano, when did you order it?"

"A year ago."

Chief Maxwell frowned. "Why does it take a year to get a piano?"

Piper sighed, "Because my piano is a Steinway. It's handmade with over twelve thousand parts."

Maxwell waved his hand again. "I don't get it, but at least we have a timetable established. Walk with me, and we'll head into the hall."

"Is he . . . is he . . .?"

"The body is still there, yes. Do you know the deceased?"

Piper nodded. "Daniel Graves, my ex-fiancé."

Chief Maxwell let out a low whistle. "Why didn't anyone tell me?"

"You didn't ask?" Piper cringed, waiting for him to yell or blame her for her answer.

"Never mind. Stay here. I'll be right back—and we start from the beginning this time."

He hurried out of the office, and Piper waited at her desk, her heart pounding. She grabbed the little green frog and rolled it in her hands. "Where did you come from? You sure picked a bad day to show up. We're in a lot of trouble, Mr. Little Green Frog." Piper sighed and laid her head on her desk.

After several hours of grilling by the chief, Piper pulled into the driveway of her fixer-upper Victorian home. She parked her Mercedes next to her mother's BMW as the final peaceful strains of Debussy's "Arabesque" washed over her. One of her senior students prepared this piece for the recital. She sighed and gathered items from the passenger seat.

"Mom?" Piper called. "What are you doing here?"

Sarah Haydn walked down the hall, wiping her hands on a towel. "Making supper for you. I knew you needed food after your recital." Her mom smiled and pulled her into a hug.

"Hmmm. Sweetheart—you're so tense. It didn't go well? Did someone forget their piece?" Sarah turned back to the kitchen. "Come. Sit down and eat."

The basil and garlic in her mom's famous Capellini Pomodoro drifted to Piper. Her stomach lurched. *I cannot eat.*

"Sit." Piper's mother pointed to the stool at the counter and dished up plates of pasta. Sarah Haydn remained young and beautiful, and people often mistook her for Piper's sister instead of her mom. Her blonde hair remained perfectly styled, even with steam from the pasta swirling around her face. Sarah Haydn always appeared fresh from a photoshoot—impeccable and chic.

"Mom, didn't you hear?"

"Hmmm . . . I knew about your recital. What else?" Sarah paused, holding the pot of pasta above the counter. She tilted her head and frowned. "Something with your brothers? I don't know." She sat across from Piper and smiled. "Let's pray."

They bowed their heads, and Sarah thanked the Lord for their food. She smiled at Piper. "Well, what did I miss?"

Piper took a deep breath and said, "My Steinway came today—"

"Yes," Sarah said, interrupting. "I'm so sorry. I meant to come over and listen to you test the piano before the recital. Tell me about it. Is it beautiful? Sound good? Fit well on the stage?"

"Mom." Piper interrupted. "Daniel Graves was in the piano."

Sarah Haydn stopped chewing and frowned. "Daniel Graves works at Notes? Didn't he work at some fancy office? When did he get a job delivering pianos?"

"Mother, you are not listening to me. My Steinway came this afternoon, and when they opened it, Daniel Graves was inside the piano crate."

Her mother frowned. "That man is so odd, Piper. I'm glad he didn't marry you. What's he thinking of showing up and ruining your important day? Daniel Graves is a jerk. I'm glad you've seen his true colors." She stood to refill her water glass. "You need a refill?"

"Mother—stop. I'm trying to tell you Daniel Graves is dead. We found his *body* in my Steinway."

Sarah turned to Piper, dropping her glass. The crystal goblet shattered on Piper's tile floor, tinkling like tiny bells. "Honey, what in the world?" Her mother hurried around the counter, pulling Piper into a hug. "Oh, honey!" she murmured.

Piper leaned on her mother's shoulder, inhaling the scent of Chanel's Gardenia. She took several deep breaths, her eyes closed. Mom smelled of peace.

Without warning, a sob escaped. Piper had held herself together all day. She had held herself together since Daniel ran out of the church on their wedding day. For months Piper kept her chin up and held herself together, but she fell apart, resting on her mom's shoulder, safe in her mother's embrace. She gasped, and a cry tore through the silent kitchen from deep in her soul. The intensity of the wail surprised Piper, but she couldn't hold back. She cried for lost dreams and the ugly memory of Daniel's body inside the piano.

"Oh, Mom." She sobbed, hiccupping.

Sarah Haydn held Piper and patted her back, murmuring, "Let it out, baby."

"Oh, Mom—his eyes . . . " She couldn't talk over the lump in her throat. She lay against her mom's shoulder, trying to focus on the print of her mother's blouse—anything to force herself to calm down.

Haydns didn't fall apart or give in to their emotions. Piper had resolved to pull herself together, but her resolve disappeared when Mom pulled her close. The Haydns loved each other, but they bottled emotions and hid negative feelings.

Piper took deep breaths to calm herself. "I'm ruining your blouse," she whispered.

Her mom leaned back, grabbed the hem of her blouse, and wiped Piper's eyes. "No one cares about my blouse. Take a drink." She handed Piper a glass of water and organized the food in the refrigerator. "You're coming home with me. I'm not leaving you alone, and your father needs to know what's going on. Get your shoes. I'll send someone to clean this kitchen tomorrow, but you need your mommy for now. Let's go."

Walking to the car felt like wading through deep water. Piper's joints and muscles ached. Her stuffed head pounded, and her nose dripped. Her swollen eyes itched, her ears rang, and sobs lurked beneath the surface. "I'm a mess, Mother."

"A good hot bath and a cup of tea will help. Get in the car." Sarah unlocked the door. Piper dropped into the passenger seat, and her mother closed the door. When Sarah shifted the car in reverse, headlights shone behind them.

"Who is that?"

Piper sighed. "Rosie said she wanted to come over."

"I'll tell her to come over to our house in the morning. You're in no condition to talk to anyone right now. Best friend or not."

Sarah rolled the window down. "Rosie, come to our house tomorrow. I'm . . ."

Chief Maxwell stared into the window. "Ladies, I need to speak with Piper. Step out of the car, please."

Sarah sputtered and frowned. "Sir, I'm sure you understand my daughter's endured a difficult day. She'll speak with you in the morning."

"I understand, but I still need to speak with Miss Haydn."

"Does she need a lawyer?" Sarah asked.

"Mom—stop." Piper opened her door and stepped out of the car. "Chief Maxwell?"

"I have a search warrant for your home and academy." He handed her papers and motioned behind him. Several officers stepped out of the shadows and walked toward her house.

Sarah jumped out of the car. "What's this?"

"Search warrant, ma'am."

"Get in the car, Piper—I'm calling your father," Sarah ordered.

Piper's mind swam, and she couldn't focus. The control she craved slipped away with each second.

Chief Maxwell walked away, and Piper resisted the urge to run after him screaming. She wanted to yell, "You've got it all wrong! I didn't do it!" But screaming at a police officer would cause problems she didn't have the strength to handle. Chief Maxwell wouldn't care about her opinions or feelings anyway.

She plopped into the passenger seat and rested her head on the dashboard. "Could this day get any worse?" she said with a groan.

Piper waited in her mom's car, concentrating on her breath. She had to calm down. Throbbing pain in the back of her neck warned of an impending headache. She closed her eyes, listening to her mom's phone call.

"What did Dad say?"

"Dad says to come home, and he'll call the attorney to come over to your house and lock up when they finish."

"Are we allowed to leave?"

"You know we've been through this with your brother. The warrants aren't for you. They're for searching your property."

"What do they hope to find, Mom?"

"Did you search killing methods on one of your computers?"

"Mom!" Piper shouted. "That's not funny. Don't say something so awful."

Sarah frowned. "I can't say Daniel didn't deserve it, but I wish he had died without ruining your piano."

Piper covered her eyes and ran her hand down her face blowing out a breath. "That's a good way to get someone arrested, Mother."

Sarah smiled and patted Piper's arm. "Don't worry. I won't say it to those officers in there."

"Don't say it to *anyone.*"

Piper's phone rang. "Rosie, where are you?"

"Down the street. What's with all the cops?"

"Can you meet me at Mom and Dad's house? I'll explain."

"Okey-dokey. See you in a few."

Sarah Haydn shifted the car in reverse. "Buckle up, dear," she said.

Piper gazed out the window as the town went past.

What does everyone think about this mess? Do people believe me capable of murder? Her stomach lurched, remembering the sight of Daniel's body. *I couldn't hurt anyone. Sure, I was angry, but . . .*

"Piper Grace, I have a question for you, and I don't want you to get angry at me," her mother said. "Did you kill that man?"

Piper's cheeks burned, and she sighed. "Oh, Mom."

"I know I shouldn't ask, but if I ask now, I won't doubt later," Sarah said.

"I *couldn't* kill him," Piper said in a low voice.

Sarah's head snapped around. "Did you still love that man? After what he did to you? Oh, Piper. I thought you were smarter than that."

Piper heard her mother's disappointment simmering under the surface. Her parents loved her, but she wasn't enough—she didn't quite fit the Haydn mold. She had failed her parents by going into music rather than the family's orchard business. Piper held back tears—surprised she had any left after this terrible day.

"I did still love Daniel, Mom. I know it's ridiculous. I didn't want to reestablish a relationship with him, but I missed him—or at least the person I assumed he was."

"He was GQ for sure." Sarah giggled.

"Mother, this is serious—not something to laugh about."

"I know, sweetheart. It's awful, and I'm angry for you, but I can't muster any sorrow for Daniel Graves. If that means I'm a horrible person, then so be it. He hurt my little girl, and I don't tolerate jerks mistreating my children." She reached over and patted Piper's leg. "I'll behave in front of the police. Don't worry."

"Well, you have to behave in front of *everyone*—no repeating what you said in this car. You'll get me in trouble. That's not what you want, is it?" Piper crossed her arms and glared at her mother.

"Of course not. Let's get you home and settled. I don't want you and Rosie talking all night as you used to do when you were little girls."

"I don't think I can do anything *but* sleep. I'm exhausted."

"I'll bring tea up for you. A cup of chamomile should help you settle in and rest. Things will seem better in the morning. Promise."

Piper smiled. Things would not seem better in the morning, but tonight she would rest and pretend that when the sun rose she would find herself back in her normal life.

Piper lay on the bed in her old room. The moment her head hit the pillow, a yawn escaped.

"Tired?" Rosie asked.

"I'm worse than tired. But I don't know if I can sleep." Piper shook her head, trying to clear the image of Daniel in her piano.

"Did you ever meet Daniel's family, Piper?"

"No, why?"

"I don't know. Don't you think it's odd none of his family came to the wedding?"

"He said they weren't close, and he didn't need their approval."

Rosie wrinkled her nose. "It's weird. That's all I'm saying."

"I quit trying to figure it out."

"Did it mess you up?" Rosie asked. "I know you were sad and angry. But inside? Do you still think about him?"

Piper tossed the covers off and sat on the side of the bed. "Yes. I've wondered what I did to chase him away. He never called or answered my emails. I've never seen him again since the day he left me in front of a packed church."

Rosie let out a whistle. "I didn't want to ask you about him, but now . . ." She waved her hands in the air. "I figured it didn't matter. Did you question God?"

"You could have asked me anytime, Rosie. You know that, and yes—I did struggle with my faith."

"I can see that. 'Why would You let this happen to me?' Right?"

Piper nodded. "That, and I prayed about marrying him, Rosie. I prayed for a long time before I said yes. I didn't want to fall in love with the wrong man." She smiled a small crooked smile. "Failed that test."

"He didn't deserve you, Piper Haydn. God will bring someone. I know it."

"I'm not looking, Rosie. I'm going to stay an old maid in my big old fixer-upper house. I'll get a cat and take up knitting."

Rosie fell on the bed giggling. "You're so funny. You're the furthest thing from an old maid there is."

"Well, Roosevelt, we are both old maids, so better learn to deal with it."

Rosie threw a pillow at Piper. "Speak for yourself, Piper. I'm nothing of the sort."

"Rosie?"

"Hmmm."

"I'm going to figure out who did this. You in?"

"You mean Nancy Drew stuff?"

"Exactly. We'll figure out where to start in the morning. I have to get some sleep now, but we have a lot to sort through tomorrow."

Rosie giggled and turned out the light. "Night, Nancy," she whispered.

CHAPTER TWO

Wednesday

S un streamed through the bedroom window, waking Piper. She stretched and frowned. *Why am I at Mom and Dad's?* When she glanced over to the other bed and saw Rosie, the horror of the day before hit in an overwhelming wave. She clutched her stomach and groaned. *Everything hurts. Lord, how am I going to do this?* She sighed and nudged Rosie. "Hey—wake up."

Rosie rolled over and threw her arm over her eyes. "Who left the curtain open? Ugh."

"Come on. We have a lot to do today, starting with writing a list of suspects."

Rosie didn't move. Her curls spread across the pillow, a frown on her face.

Piper poked her arm. "Rosie, we're never going to solve this mess if you stay in bed."

"Your bed is so comfortable, Piper. Why did you ever move out? I'd never leave home if this were my bed." She rolled to the wall, pulling the blanket over her face. "Five more minutes."

"I'm going down to find something to eat. Meet me on the sunporch in ten?" She nudged Rosie's snoozing form. *"Okay?"*

"Okay. Okay. I'll get up. Don't eat all the sugar cereal before I come down."

"My mother doesn't buy sugar cereal, Rosie. Hurry up now. I can't go to the academy today, and we have to work on this list together. Get your thinking cap on while you roll out of bed. My brain is a cluttered mess. I'm gonna need yours."

Rosie groaned.

Chief Maxwell had informed her that the academy remained off-limits—at least for today. Piper couldn't hold off on parent calls and paperwork, but she must first find food and coffee. At least she would get a good cup of coffee this morning. Her mother loved coffee more than Piper did, and Mom's own coffee bar rivaled the coffee shops.

Piper yawned and pushed open the kitchen door. *Oh, no!* Her entire family was sitting at the long table with Dad's attorney, Lenny. "Whoa . . . I didn't expect a crowd!"

She tugged her T-shirt down and grabbed the elastic off her wrist to pull her blonde hair into a ponytail. "Wait for me. I'll run upstairs and get presentable."

"No time, Piper. Come—join us." Her father pushed papers aside and stood to pull out a chair. "We called a meeting of The Core."

Piper grimaced. Her father called family meetings "The Core" to discuss orchard decisions—buying, selling, and spending charitable trust funds. Her brother Chase's escapades and scrapes with the law also forced several meetings of The Core.

Chase eyed her from the end of the table and smirked. "Well, well, well—never expected a meeting of The Core for precious Piper."

"Chase," Jack Haydn said, his voice carrying the warning tone Piper recognized from childhood.

Chase rolled his eyes, pointed at Piper, then back at himself and winked.

Piper loved her little brother, but somehow he seemed to get into enough trouble for the whole family. *How does he get away with it? There's no room for getting into trouble in this family.* The Haydn children represented their family in Cranberry Harbor, and her parents expected them to behave above reproach.

Piper slid into the chair next to her mother. Sarah wore a sleeveless blouse with a floppy bow at the neck, a triple strand of pearls, and perfect makeup. Piper glanced down to see her mother's full skirt and ballet flats next to her bare legs and blushed.

I am clearly underdressed.

Her brother Braden sat across the table, wearing a suit and tie as Father and Lenny did.

Piper wanted to crawl under the table. She had never appeared at meetings of The Core in her pajamas. "Why didn't anyone tell me to dress for a meeting?" She heard the whine in her voice and sat up straight, attempting to appear an essential family member. She cleared her throat and glanced around the table with a smile. "I mean, if I had known, I would have come down earlier."

Dad's secretary stepped to his side placing papers next to his coffee cup.

Coffee. She took a deep breath. *If I get up now to brew a cup of coffee, Dad will get upset.*

"Too much to accomplish to wait for you to decide to roll out of bed, Piper Grace. It's already 8:30." Her father raised his eyebrows and stared. She smiled a tiny smile but clamped her lips shut before a sigh escaped.

"As I said," Jack continued, "Lenny will handle all comments to the press. You will not speak to reporters or answer phone calls from any of them. Is that clear?" Dad peered over his glasses and glanced around the table. Everyone nodded.

What else had they agreed to in my absence?

"Piper, Lenny locked your home last night when the officers finished. It's quite a mess, so I'll send a cleaning crew this afternoon.

You will stay here until everything settles down. Reporters caught wind of the story, and they're waiting at the end of your driveway."

Piper sighed and rubbed the back of her neck. She loved her parents, and their lavish home was spacious and comfortable, but she wanted to escape to her "in need of repair" Victorian home. She longed for her private space.

"I want to get home as soon as possible. . . ." She trailed off at the warning look her father flashed her way.

"Braden will accompany you home to pick up anything you need, Piper." Jack Haydn smiled at his oldest son.

Piper nodded, but her throat thickened and her head pounded. *I'm a grown woman, but this feels like a punishment for stealing cookies from the kitchen.*

The scent of coffee tormented her groggy brain. She needed caffeine soon to endure any more of this meeting. She glanced around the table and pointed at Chase's iced coffee. He smirked and passed the glass down the table. She took a big sip and exhaled. *Happiness.*

When she glanced around the table, everyone stared.

"Piper?" Lenny said.

"I . . . I'm sorry. Can you repeat that?" Piper blushed.

"I asked if you needed anything at the academy today."

She frowned and tapped her lips. "I don't believe so. I may need to grab paperwork tomorrow."

"Fine," the attorney said. "If you need to enter the academy for any reason, I will go with you. Do not go alone."

She nodded. "How long will the investigation last?"

"They haven't said. The officers collected the body this morning about an hour ago."

Piper blanched. "He was there this whole time?"

"These things take time, Piper," Jack said as he shuffled papers. "We are set for the day. Does everyone understand their responsibilities? Chase?" he fixed a stare on his son at the end of the table.

"Aye aye, Captain." Chase saluted their father.

Piper bit her lip, waiting for Jack to say something, but Chase escaped a reprimand for his impertinence.

Rosie rushed through the door and yelped.

Chase jumped up and ran to her, giving her a bear hug. "Rosie—long time no see!" He twirled her around and set her on the floor. "I didn't know you were here."

Rosie smiled and pushed away from Chase. "Nice to see you too, Chase. What did I interrupt?" She grimaced, pretending to hide her face behind her hands.

Jack Haydn stood and picked up the sheaf of papers. "Nothing, Rosie. We're wrapping up right now. Grab some coffee and let the cook know if you want something for breakfast." He stepped to her and gave her a small peck on the cheek. "Good to see you. It's been too long."

Rosie smiled. "Oh, you know me. I'm here, there, and everywhere." Rosie glanced at Piper and hurried from the room.

Braden pulled Piper into a hug. "I'm sorry, Piper. Are you holding up?"

Tears stung her eyes. "No, Braden—I am not."

"Hang in there. Between Dad and Lenny and your brothers, you're going to survive this." He squeezed her shoulder and stepped away.

Her mother pulled her into a comforting hug. "Your father's worried about you, and he has other things going on at the orchard. He's frustrated. Don't let his stiffness bother you. Everything will work out."

Piper pasted on a fake smile. *Yes. Everything would work out. Right? It has to.*

"Please, God," she whispered. "I need to solve this murder and get back to my peaceful life."

Piper brewed a latte at her mom's coffee bar, inhaling the coffee beans' aroma while she waited. Braden said he would pick her up after lunch to gather anything she needed from her house. *I need calm to solve this mess.*

Piper popped into her dad's office and grabbed a notebook and pen from his desk. She hurried to the sunroom to write a suspect list.

The sunroom sat at the back of the house overlooking the yard and a stone fence surrounding the Haydn property. Piper loved this room as a child and spent countless hours curled up in the corner of the couch reading. She settled onto the overstuffed chair and stared out the window overlooking her mom's prized roses. The flowers bloomed in an explosion of pinks and reds, and Piper stepped to the door and took several deep breaths of the fragrance. She tried to still her racing mind.

"Lord," she whispered, "can you please help me? I don't know what to do, and murder seems too big. But I need to figure out who did this and get my academy opened. I need to know what happened to Daniel. Please."

She shut the door and curled up in the chair, sipping her latte, trying to decide where to look for clues. She scribbled several ideas before Rosie bounded in.

"There you are. I forgot to check in here. Why aren't you playing the piano?"

"Not today. Playing the piano seems. . . ." she trailed off and shuddered.

"What are you working on?" Rosie leaned over the back of Piper's chair.

Piper sighed. "I'm trying to write a list of who to talk to or where to start."

"You're serious about figuring this out by yourself?"

Piper nodded. "Not by myself. You'll help, right?"

"Of course." Rosie plopped onto the couch across from Piper. "Where should we start?"

"I'm trying to decide, and I don't know. What do you think?"

Rosie sighed. "What about a 'whodunit' list?"

Piper pulled out the notebook and her father's expensive Urushi pen she had grabbed from his desk. "Let's start with suspects."

"Did the police say anything yet?"

"Nothing."

"Okay," Rosie said. "Let's concentrate. . . . Who worked with Daniel?"

"I don't know. I didn't meet anyone except at the office party last Christmas."

"Think," Rosie said. She reached over and grabbed Piper's latte and gulped the warm liquid. Piper raised her eyebrows at her friend.

Rosie grinned. "What? I'm in my pajamas. I couldn't stick around and brew myself a coffee." She took a big sip and grinned. Rosie wiped the foam off her lip with the back of her hand and winked at Piper.

"Coworkers," Piper said. "Who else?"

"It can't be a generic coworker, Piper. You have to name names. Who was at the party?"

Piper leaned her head back and closed her eyes, searching her memories of the Christmas party. "His secretary kept staring at me funny."

"Write her down. Who else? Fancy pen, by the way."

"It's Dad's. You know, one of the guys said something weird. When we got there, he seemed surprised. He pulled Daniel aside and said, 'Another one, huh?' Then Daniel laughed, and they slapped each other on the back."

Rosie tapped her lips with her finger. "Is that suspicious? I mean, it's weird, but I don't know what it means."

"I'll write it down. I had forgotten about that."

"You didn't think about a lot of things." Rosie sighed.

"What do you mean?" Piper tilted her head and frowned.

"I don't know, Piper. Daniel seemed nice and everything, but something was always off." She waved her hand. "We can't change the past. I shouldn't have mentioned it. Back to the list."

Piper sighed and rubbed her temple. "Solving this will take us forever."

"It's all we have right now, so let's not give up yet," Rosie said.

Piper tapped the notebook with the pen thinking through people she had met while dating Daniel. "His housekeeper," she said, scribbling the name on the list.

"Why her?"

"It's a *he*," Piper said. "Kristoff did Daniel's personal stuff and kept the house clean. He never seemed to care for Daniel. Always questioning him and acting annoyed."

"Write him down," Rosie said. "We're making progress."

"We have three names, Rosie. That's not much progress."

"How did Nancy Drew do this?" Rosie sighed.

"Someone wrote the script for her." Piper said.

"Let's find someone to do that for us."

Piper tried to hold back the giggle that bubbled up, but the sound escaped with a sob.

Rosie jumped from the couch and wrapped her arms around Piper. "Oh, Piper. I'm sorry. This is hard."

Piper dabbed her eyes. "Thanks. I keep seeing his face." Another sob escaped, and she blew out a breath, willing herself to stop. "I'm fine. Back to the list." Piper grabbed the notebook, willing her brain to identify suspects.

"You," Rosie said.

"What?"

"Write *yourself* down," she said.

"Myself? Rosie, what in the world? I didn't do this."

"I know you didn't, and *you* know you didn't, but you know everyone is thinking it. Write yourself down, and we will work on clearing you too."

"My goodness," Piper said with a huff. "How am I going to get through a murder investigation? I couldn't have killed Daniel. He's twice my size. How would I get him in that crate?"

"Perfect cover, they'd say. Adrenaline? Anger?"

Piper sighed. "You watch too many crime shows."

Rosie waggled her eyebrows and flipped her red curls with a smile. "That's why I'm here to help. You know you need my expertise."

Piper tapped the pen on the notebook, running names through her mind. "If we're going to write down wild theories, solving the murder will take forever."

"I've got all day," Rosie said. "I can't go to work anyway."

"I hear your boss will still pay you." Piper smiled.

"Good to know, boss. Write Chase down."

"Chase? Rosie, what are you saying?" Piper stared at Rosie and frowned.

"Well, come on, Piper. Chase always gets in trouble—he's not a straight arrow. He loves you and seems very protective of you. He was angry at the wedding. I saw his face when Daniel ran down the aisle."

"Smoking pot and getting arrested for public drunkenness aren't the same as murder, Rosie. Chase has his issues, but murder is a stretch."

"Add Braden too."

"Rosie, stop! My brothers didn't take out my ex."

"Do you *know* they didn't? What if they worked together? All I'm saying is I saw their faces when that man left you at the altar, and they are capable."

"They wouldn't have ruined my piano or jeopardized my business," Piper said.

Rosie waved her hands in the air. "Heat of the moment, Piper. People don't think rationally."

Piper frowned. "I'm not writing down my brothers."

"We can't clear them if you don't. Give me the notebook, and I'll write the names."

Piper grabbed the pen and scribbled her brother's names on the list. "Happy?"

Rosie smiled. "Supremely." She winked, and Piper threw the notebook at her friend.

Rosie bent to grab it, and Sarah carried in two steaming mugs.

"Lattes for you ladies. What are you up to?" She set the mugs on the coffee table and glanced at Piper's notebook.

"Trying to figure out who did this." Piper rubbed her eyes.

"Write your father and me down," Sarah said.

"Mom. Be serious. I can't write you down."

"Well, you should, honey, because we couldn't stand that man." She kissed Piper on the head and turned to leave.

"Oh, Chief Maxwell called and said he's stopping by to talk to you again in about an hour. You might want to change out of your pajamas before then."

"Write down the hunky officer," Rosie said.

"Who?"

"Chief Maxwell. He's gorgeous. I think he's secretly in love with you and wants you to notice him."

"Good grief, Rosie. You're crazy. I never saw the man before yesterday." Piper rolled her eyes.

"He *is* hunky, isn't he?" Rosie winked.

"I didn't notice." Piper shut the notebook and unfolded her legs from the chair. "I have to get dressed before he gets here. Are you staying all day?" She wrapped her hands around the warm mug and took a sip.

"No. I better get home. I'll check on you later. Wear something cute for Officer Hunky." Rosie winked.

"You're incorrigible," Piper said.

"And you love me just the way I am." Rosie bounced her curls and skipped from the room.

Piper sat in the silent room, trying to untangle her snarled brain.

She stood and blew out a breath. *I don't know what to do or think, but someone needs to fix this mess before Daniel's murder ruins my life.*

Piper grabbed the scarf her mother had bought her at the Getty Museum and tied it around her ponytail. The soft silk fabric mimicked Van Gogh's *Starry Night.* She hadn't taken time to match the clothing she packed last night, but she dressed quickly, hoping to pass as presentable. *This nightmare has to end—soon.*

When Piper tapped her phone, Debussy's "La Mer" filled the room. She switched the music off and sighed. Choosing Debussy seemed like a good idea when she planned the recital. Now she worried she would never enjoy his music again.

She brushed her teeth, wondering whose name to add to the list of suspects. The face of her secretary, Lisa, flitted through her mind, and Piper frowned.

Lisa? Now I'm suspecting decent people.

Lisa, a single mother of two preteen children, worked hard and kept Piper's office organized. Piper trusted her with the receipts and bank deposits, and Lisa never gave her a reason to worry about anything. She was an excellent employee and made Piper look good. Still, Piper couldn't shake the uneasy feeling. She sighed, walked over to the notebook, and scribbled, "Lisa."

There—you happy?

She tucked the notebook into her bag and went to see if Chief Maxwell waited, hoping he would forget his appointment. She needed more caffeine. Her head pounded, and her eyes drooped.

He will suspect me if I sit there looking like the cat drug me in at midnight.

Piper found the kitchen empty and tapped her fingers on the countertop while waiting for her coffee to brew. The cupboard above the coffee bar overflowed with cups from around the world. Piper grabbed a thick pottery mug her mother had brought home from their trip to London a couple of years ago and filled it with steaming coffee. She opened the small fridge under the bar to find cream and poured a thick dollop into her mug. She settled at the table to sip the coffee in peace and grabbed her phone.

One hundred forty-seven text messages and fifteen voice mails. Countless emails filled the inbox, but she couldn't deal with returning messages at the moment.

The most recent messages were from Trefor.

--Hey. U ok?

--Call me?

--Trying not to worry. Let me know if I can help.

                                                    --I'm ok. Thanks.

She scrolled through the other messages to see that Ruby checked in, along with several parents and other business owners. Piper set the phone on the table and sighed.

So much to do, but this interview stood in her way. She would figure out a way to work through everything else after talking to Chief Maxwell.

While waiting, Piper thought of her hometown. Cranberry Harbor, Wisconsin—population 4,786—set on the shore of Glacier Lake in north-central Wisconsin. The small town, always humming with activity, was the perfect place to live—or at least it was before yesterday.

The cranberry industry and the lake brought in tourists, and the whole town thrived. Jack Haydn had helped revitalize the downtown business district by having the orchard sponsor festivals and pay for the fireworks display. Sarah served on several boards overseeing the planning and rebuilding of the business district. Their plan had worked—the tiny town became a year-round destination—the perfect getaway for Midwesterners wanting to escape their busy cities and return to life at a slower pace.

Piper frequented the downtown businesses, happy to support her friends. She loved to shop at The Kindred Spirits Book Shoppe and visit Dominique at the Sweetberry Bakery. Her mom loved the Wooly Llama Yarn Store, and Jack stopped at Tea Thyme for his morning cup of Earl Grey. The Haydn family's love of Cranberry Harbor made Piper proud to open her academy and join the area businesses. She wanted to take part in revitalizing the area.

But now.

She leaned her head on her hands and took a deep breath, trying to banish the image of Daniel's face in her Steinway.

"Miss Haydn?"

Piper startled at the man's voice. "Chief Maxwell." She held out her hand. "My attorney will join us if you don't mind waiting. Do you care for coffee?"

He dropped his notebook onto the table and sat in Jack's spot.

"Nothing, thank you," he answered.

Lenny ran in huffing and sat across from Piper. "Sorry—busy morning."

Chief Maxwell opened the notebook. "Miss Haydn, we removed the body this morning, and now we wait for toxicology and autopsy results. The turnaround time in Madison is rather lengthy. I'll keep you posted." He nodded at Lenny. "We should have the building back in your hands by this evening as long as we collect everything we need. You'll want to arrange a cleaning crew. I don't know what you'll want to do with the . . ." He trailed off and cleared his throat.

"Piano?" Piper asked.

He nodded.

"I'll call the music store. They'll need to remove it. Did you have any questions for me?"

Chief Maxwell rested his elbows on the table and leaned forward.

Piper glanced at the gray hair curling at his temple and wondered how old he was. She blinked to clear her thoughts before she said something foolish.

"Miss Haydn, do you have any idea who would murder Daniel Graves?"

"I don't. I wracked my brain all night. I don't remember Daniel having enemies."

"We went over your relationship last night, but did you think of anyone who wanted to hurt him because he hurt you?"

She shook her head, hoping he couldn't see anything in her expression. She willed herself to keep quiet before she blurted out any of the names on her list.

"No, Chief Maxwell, I can't think of anyone I know who'd murder Daniel Graves and stuff him into my brand-new Steinway. It's a ridiculous, horrible thing. I don't hang around with people capable of murder."

Chief Maxwell stared at her for a moment, then shut his notebook. "Don't leave town. I'll have more questions, I'm sure." He handed Piper his contact information and gave a card to Lenny. "Call me if you think of anything I should know."

"Have you notified his family?"

"Yes, we talked to his wife this morning," Chief Maxwell said.

A jolt ran through Piper, and she stared at the man. "Um . . . what? What did you say?" She stammered.

"I said we notified his wife this morning."

The coffee in Piper's stomach rumbled, and she gripped the table. She scratched her cheek and tilted her head. Her eyebrows rose, and her voice squeaked. "Excuse me. Did you say *wife*?"

"I assumed you knew." Chief Maxwell stared at her, his eyebrows raised.

"How would I know that? I was going to marry the man. I didn't know he was married." She took a deep breath. "How long were they married?"

Chief Maxwell flipped through his notebook and said, "Twenty-two years." He snapped it shut. "I figure that's why he jilted you—better that than bigamy." He left the room, and Lenny opened his mouth.

Piper held up her hand. "Not now, Lenny. I'm about to get sick."

She ran from the room. *Can a person hyperventilate and throw up at the same time? Because I'm going to do both.*

Piper fled to the conservatory, dropped onto the piano bench, and banged her hands on the keys. When her heartbeat slowed, she played. Her fingers flew over the keys, pounding out her shock and sadness. Playing the piano was her coping mechanism and stress release. For a brief moment yesterday, she doubted she would ever touch a piano again without seeing Daniel's face. But today her heart flooded with gratitude that she played without picturing his dead body.

Piper allowed the music to empty her mind while playing Vivaldi's "Summer Presto" from the Four Seasons several times, then moved to Beethoven's "Rage over a Lost Penny." She poured her heart into the music, allowing the pieces to carry her mind to places where people didn't find dead bodies in their brand-new pianos. After pounding out the music, her stress melted, and she played one of her favorites—Chopin's "Raindrops." Her mind calmed, and her body relaxed.

"Bravo." Braden sat in the chair near the door.

"How long have you been there?" she demanded. Her cheeks flushed, and she fiddled with the buttons on her skirt. She had poured way too much emotion into her playing.

What had Braden seen?

"Long enough."

"Why didn't you interrupt me?"

He laughed. "Oh, no, little sister. I learned long ago that one does not interrupt Miss Piper Grace when she's at the piano." He stood and kissed the top of her head.

"Well, you could have cleared your throat or something to let me know you were here."

He raised his eyebrows. "And miss the performance? No way. You ready to go?"

"Let me grab my purse. I'll be right back."

She hurried upstairs to get her clothes, happy that her time at the piano had cleared her mind. She would tell Braden to leave her at her house. She needed to be in her own space to deal with the stress. She wasn't a child anymore, no matter how her parents viewed her.

Piper second-guessed her decision to stay home when they drove through the crowd of reporters camped at the end of her driveway. She wouldn't answer the door, but she would stay home—she had made up her mind.

Braden walked her inside and shut the door. "Man, Piper—you need to fix this place up a bit."

Piper sighed. "Yes, Braden. I know. It's an old house, and it needs a lot of love."

"It needs a lot of something—that's for sure." He laughed. "A big old wrecking ball, I'd say."

"You stop now. I love this old place." She patted the doorpost and in a stage whisper said, "Don't listen to him. I love you."

Braden rolled his eyes. "You're a nut. Grab your stuff, and I'll get you back to Mom and Dad's."

"I'm staying here, Braden."

His eyes widened. "Oh, no, you're not. The Core decided you're staying with Mom and Dad 'til the investigation is over."

"I don't care what The Core decided. I will stay here. I'm an adult, Braden." She crossed her arms, prepared for a fight with her goody-two-shoes older brother, who never went against their father's wishes.

He blew out a low whistle. "Okay, Sis, but you're telling Dad because I'm not going anywhere near that mess. You sure?"

She nodded.

"All righty then." He gave her a quick peck on the cheek. "Do not talk to reporters without Lenny. You'll at least obey *that* rule, right?"

"Of course. I'm not stupid."

He rolled his eyes and said, "Well . . ."

"Out," she said, locking the door behind her brother.

Her stomach rumbled, and she pulled the leftover pasta from the fridge.

Was that last night?

She warmed the food in the microwave, grabbed the notebook, and wrote. "Daniel's wife."

She sighed, unable to come to terms with the information. She had grieved the loss of the relationship, cataloging what she had done wrong—wondering why he never called after leaving her at the altar.

Married. Married the whole time.

Piper tapped her phone and searched online. She shivered when the first search result returned a photo of Daniel and his wife—Felicity. Piper blew out a breath and rubbed her cool hands on her flushed face.

"They're happy," she whispered and stared at the photo. Felicity was mid-forties—same age as Daniel. She stood by his side, dressed in a chic red gown, and both raised a glass. Smiles spread across their faces.

Why didn't I ever search for him before? I believed everything he told me. Hook, line, and sinker. He saw me coming a mile away with stupid *tattooed on my forehead.*

Piper sighed, remembering how she met him at the adult singles class by chance. She trusted him and believed he trusted in God.

I can't think about Daniel right now.

She drew a line through *Daniel's wife* and wrote *Felicity Graves*. She texted Rosie.

--I'm back at my house. Come over when you have time. Call first, so I don't think you're a reporter. LOL.

She scrolled through texts to see what fires she needed to extinguish and answered several messages from worried parents. She assured them of her safety and that she would reopen the academy as soon as possible.

Piper needed monthly reports printed for review and called Lisa, but her voicemail answered. She scraped leftover pasta into the trash and rinsed her dishes, trying to decide what steps to take to solve Daniel's murder. She wanted to solve the mystery and get back to her routine, but her mind was blank.

Who did this? Why?

The questions tumbled through her brain without answers. She had plopped onto her sofa to work through the puzzling situation when her phone dinged.

--Can I get u anything?

--Thanks, Trefor. I need a massive coffee from Ruby's if you want to bring it to my house.

--On my way.

Piper smiled at the text and dropped the phone onto the couch. She and Trefor worked in competing jobs—piano teachers and music classes—but they formed an easy friendship despite their different teaching methods. Piper's academy ran on a strict schedule with rules and expectations. Trefor's classes at Notes Music Centre ran like a free-range chicken ranch—anything goes. But the children loved his teaching, and everything seemed to work well for him. Piper appreciated having a musician friend to talk music shop with occasionally. She enjoyed hanging out with him, but he and Rosie butted heads.

Piper pursed her lips, trying to force her brain to solve the murder, but it didn't work. She stared at the wall and pounded her fist on the couch.

She paced, hoping the movement would jiggle something loose in her fuzzy brain.

Nope. Nothing.

She curled up in the overstuffed floral chair in the turret—her favorite room in her Victorian painted lady house—the perfect size for a sofa, a couple of chairs, and her piano. The windows surrounding the room spilled golden sunlight across the room, and she rested her head on the side of the chair. She drifted off into a fitful sleep interrupted by strange dreams and odd noises until a knock startled her. Piper forced her eyes open and screamed at the face peering into the window next to her chair.

"Oh, Trefor! You scared me!" Piper yelled. She jumped out of her chair to open the door.

"Sorry." He grinned and handed her an extra-large cup of Ruby's dark roast coffee.

Piper closed her eyes and took a deep breath inhaling the coffee scent before she drank. "Mmm. Thank you for this." She took a big sip and waved him in. "Come, sit."

"How are you today?" Trefor pulled out his hand sanitizer and slathered it into his hands. He winced. "Paper cut."

"I'm exhausted and confused, but I'm trying to hold on. You?"

Piper pretended to scratch her nose to blunt the odor of Trefor's strong sanitizer.

"My blood pressure returned to normal, but I'm still shocked."

Trefor's eyes clouded, and he glanced out the window. "Unbelievable."

She leaned over and patted his knee. "I know. It's awful. I'm trying to sort through who is capable of doing something so terrible. I . . ."

"Yeah, it's not something that happens around here. I'm still in a fog."

"I need to call your boss to have the Steinway removed. I can't keep the piano after . . ."

Trefor nodded. "Of course. Don't worry about the details. I'll take care of everything for you. You shouldn't have that stress to deal with on top of all the other issues."

Piper smiled. "That's such a help. Thank you for taking that off my plate."

Trefor had asked her out a few times before he dated Josie, but Piper had always declined. He was a nice guy but not her type. His skinny jeans and slouchy hat didn't scream "manly" to her. But then again, Mr. Manly himself—Daniel Graves—turned out to be a cheating liar. She sighed and sipped her coffee. The warm liquid helped clear the fuzzy exhaustion from her mind. "You're quiet," she said.

Trefor picked at the frayed knee on his skinny jeans and rubbed his beard. "Yeah. Sorry. It's the murder for sure. Also, a couple of weeks ago, I found out that Josie is seeing someone else without telling me she wanted to break up."

"Oh, Trefor. I'm sorry. That stinks."

"The worst part is that his name is *Trevor*. She did that on purpose to hurt me—cheat on me with a guy named Trevor? Why didn't she date a guy named Joe or Tristan? Anything else."

Piper choked back a laugh. She didn't want to minimize the hurt, but his complaint sounded funny when said aloud.

Trefor jumped from the couch, his nostrils flaring and his eyes wild. He ran his hands through his hair and gritted his teeth. "It's not funny, Piper. She broke my heart."

Piper held up her hand. "No, no, Trefor—I'm sorry. I didn't mean to laugh—it's the stress. I'm doing and saying things I'd never do and say. Please forgive me."

He sat on the edge of the couch, his hands folded, eyes closed.

"How can I help?" she asked.

"Nothing. Josie's gone, and I need to figure out how to live without her. She took the cat too. I loved that cat." Trefor sighed.

Piper wrapped her hands around the warm cup and sighed too. "It seems things go from bad to worse. That's too bad about the cat—I've wanted a cat for a while. Losing a pet would break my heart too."

He glanced up and smiled. "You want a cat? We can search at the humane society and both pick one out. I'll call and check the hours."

Piper frowned. "Now's not a good time to adopt a cat until we solve this and life settles down a bit. Right?"

"Oh. Sure, I get that. Got carried away." He smiled.

He jumped at a knock at the door. "Whoa—scared me!" He laughed.

Piper laughed. "And you weren't even asleep."

Rosie breezed in, carrying two cups of coffee. "I stopped at Ruby's and grabbed a latte. Oh. You already have coffee?" She pouted. "Hey, Trefor."

He smiled, and Piper grabbed the latte. "I'll drink it—you know me. Have a seat. Trefor brought me a cup from Ruby's, but this situation needs all the coffee in the world."

Rosie curled up in the chair opposite Piper. "What's up, Trefor? How do you feel about everything?"

He scowled. "It's awful. I mean, what's happening with the world if this can happen in Cranberry Harbor?"

"Exactly," Rosie said.

"Trefor's girlfriend broke up with him too," Piper said.

"Oh, no, Trefor! You said she was 'the one.' What happened?"

"Josie cheated on me with a guy named Trevor. I loved her, you know. I did think she was 'the one,' but Trevor must have something I don't."

"Maybe a *v* in his name," Rosie said. Her laughter burst out in a loud guffaw, her curls bouncing as she laughed. She rested her hand on her heart and took several deep breaths. "Oh, that's hilarious, Trefor."

Piper's eyes widened, and she groaned, trying to grab Rosie's attention, but Rosie laughed with her eyes closed.

Trefor stood up, spilling his coffee from his lap. "It's not funny!" he yelled as he stormed from the house, slamming the door.

"What?" Rosie asked, glancing around. "He *was* kidding, wasn't he?" She giggled.

"He wasn't." Piper mopped up the coffee. "He'll get over it soon. Come to the kitchen. Let's work on this murder."

Rosie followed and perched on a stool at the counter. "What have you figured out?"

"Daniel had a wife."

"What?" Rosie shrieked.

Piper nodded, and tears stung her eyes. "For twenty-two years." Saying it out loud broke a fragile spot in her heart, and tears flowed.

"Oh, no, Piper." Rosie wrapped her arms around her. "That jerk. If he wasn't dead, I'd kill him."

"Don't say that, Rosie," Piper whispered. "It might get you in trouble."

Rosie patted Piper's back, her bracelets jangling a tune. "Well, write me on the suspect list then."

"I don't know what to do," Piper said. "I'm ashamed. I feel that I did something sinful. I don't date married men. I didn't know."

"Of course, you didn't know—he lied to you." Rosie gritted her teeth and growled. "But you didn't cheat with him, Piper, right? You were waiting for marriage."

"Of course I was, but I still feel dirty." Piper wiped her eyes.

"Well, the first person you need to write down on the suspect list is Mrs. Graves."

"Already did—her name is Felicity."

"Aww, that's a pretty name." Rosie smiled.

"Yes, and she's beautiful. I looked them up. Why didn't I search for Daniel online?"

"Because you're a trusting soul. Who'd ever expect he'd join the singles class and troll for women? That's gross. Oh, Piper, he took advantage of you. He's the one to blame, not you. You hold your head high."

"I know," she whispered. "But it still feels slimy."

"*He's* the slimy one."

"Was."

"I'm sorry that he was slimy, but I'm glad you found out so you can quit pining for him." Rosie hopped back onto the stool, tossing her hair over her shoulder and leaning on her elbows.

"I was not *pining* for him!" Piper shouted.

Rosie rolled her eyes. "Whatever. What's that delicious smell?" She sniffed the air.

"My mom's Capellini Pomodoro. I warmed mine up before Trefor stopped."

"Warm me up some, girlfriend. I'm famished." Rosie smiled. "I love your mom's pasta. Mmm."

"What are you wearing, Rosie?" Piper asked while starting the microwave.

Rosie stood and twirled. The oversized floral caftan belted at her waist and flowed around her legs. The bright orange, green, and purple fabric hurt Piper's sensibilities. She would never wear garish clothes, but somehow Rosie pulled the look off.

"Thrift store special. It's from the '70s. I'm going to cut some off the bottom and sew a scarf. You want one?" Rosie asked, pointing to Piper's Van Gogh scarf.

Piper grimaced. "Uh, no thanks, Rosie."

"You should go thrifting with me," Rosie said over bites of the pasta.

Piper wrinkled her nose.

"Come on. I find great stuff. I mean, where else can I find a dress this fantastic? Right?"

Piper smiled and rolled her eyes. She pulled out the notebook. "Who else should we add?"

Rosie waved her fork and pointed at the list. "His wife must have family or friends who'd be angry at him. Did they have kids?"

Piper's face paled. "Oh, man. I don't know."

"Google." Rosie grabbed her phone to punch in a search. "None that pop up."

"Have you heard from Lisa today?"

"Nope," Rosie said. "I texted her, and she never replied."

"That's odd. Lisa didn't return my call either."

"I need your mom to cook for me more often," Rosie said as she licked sauce off the plate and wiped her chin. She grinned when she glanced up into Piper's stare. "What? It's so good."

Piper smiled. "Rosie, you're a crazy woman."

Rosie flounced her curls. "Yes, ma'am—I sure am." She rinsed her plate and rested her hands on her hips. "We have to get serious about the list and talk to people, or we'll never solve this murder."

"Let's talk to his housekeeper before adding any more names," Piper said.

"Get your keys, girl. I'm driving." Rosie hopped off the stool and skipped to the door with Piper close behind.

Piper ducked down when Rosie backed past the reporters and ignored their shouted questions.

"Miss Haydn, what does your father think of this?"

"Are you a suspect?"

Flashes clicked, and the shouts rang in her ears, but she kept her head down. "They think I'm guilty because I won't answer their questions." Piper sighed.

"Don't worry about the reporters. They're trying to make money—reporters will say anything. Where are we going?" Rosie asked.

Piper entered the address of Daniel's apartment into the GPS and settled in for the ride. "What questions should we ask when we get there?"

"How am I supposed to know? I've never been a detective before. You're the one who read all the mysteries when we were growing up. What would Nancy Drew do?" Rosie shrugged.

Piper grinned. "I guess we start by asking Kristoff when he saw Daniel last and if he remembers anything odd or any strangers hanging around."

"Sounds good to me. Write 'em down." Rosie punched the button for the radio in time to hear the news.

Police are questioning the daughter of Jack Haydn, owner of Haydn Orchards, in the murder of an area businessman Daniel Graves. The police have yet to hold a press conference, and no one from the Haydn family has made a statement. People ask if Haydn's money and influence reach into the halls of justice because, at this point, we have no new information. Stay tuned for our broadcast this evening."

Piper switched off the radio and groaned. "If our money and influence reached that far, I wouldn't have found a body in my Steinway."

"People are ridiculous. Don't let their speculation bother you. If they faced this, they wouldn't talk to the press either, and they'd want privacy. You're no different."

"Yeah, well, when your family has money, you're expected to give up your privacy." Piper leaned her head on the seat, closing her eyes.

"Wanna run away? Go to Tahiti?"

Piper smiled. "What would I do without you, Rosie Hale?"

Rosie laughed and said, "Live a boring life, I guess." She turned the radio on, switching it to her favorite station. Guitar music and a twangy voice rang out—something about tea and a grandma.

Piper groaned. "Not country again, Rosie. My ears can't handle that—you're defiling my car."

"You hush now. This isn't country. It's a new folk band from Milwaukee—Tangled Lines. That guy on the keyboard is cute, but I hear he's married." Rosie frowned. "Anyway, the driver chooses the radio station." She grinned and shimmied to the beat of the music.

"Well, pull over then, and I'll drive," Piper said with a laugh. "Never mind—we're almost there."

When Rosie pulled into the driveway of Daniel's apartment building, Piper took a deep breath. "Let's do this."

The door opened before they knocked, and Kristoff stood in the doorway. "Piper." He nodded. "Haven't seen you for a while."

"I imagine you know why, Kristoff." Her eyes narrowed. "Why didn't you tell me Daniel had a wife?"

Kristoff shrugged. "That's not my job."

"What *is* your job?" Rosie cut in.

He raised his eyebrows and turned to Piper. "If your friend must know, Daniel pays me to keep his schedule, run his errands, and anything else he may need."

"*Paid,*" Rosie said.

Kristoff looked at both of them. "I said that already."

"You said *pays.* I said *paid.*" Rosie said.

Kristoff raised his eyebrows and glanced at Piper. "What do you need, Miss Haydn?"

"We need to ask you a few questions."

"Listen—I'm sorry Daniel didn't inform you of his marital status. You're not the first and won't be the last. Get over it." He stepped inside and pushed the door closed, but Piper stuck her foot across the threshold. He stared at her shoe.

"I'm working on getting over it, Kristoff, but I'm not here about Daniel's infidelity. If I had known, I would have stopped here weeks ago. When did you see him last?"

He frowned. "He hasn't stopped here for a week. Why does that matter?"

"Because, Kristoff, I found Daniel's body in my piano yesterday," Piper said. A wave of nausea overwhelmed her, and she slumped against the doorpost, clutching her stomach.

Kristoff stepped back, his face turning pale. "*What?*" he yelled.

"Yeah," Rosie said. "His dead body."

"No." Kristoff leaned on the other side of the door frame and clutched his chest.

"The police haven't talked to you?" Piper asked.

He frowned. "No. I . . . I . . . I have to go." He slammed the door in their faces, and the blinds snapped shut.

"That went well," Rosie said.

"I don't know. Is it odd Kristoff didn't know?"

"Write it all in the notebook. We can piece clues together after talking with more people," Rosie said.

Piper wrote the questions and answers in the notebook. "Don't you think it's odd that the police haven't talked to Kristoff? Or that he hadn't heard the news?"

Rosie tapped the steering wheel with her finger for a moment. "Hmmm . . . that *is* odd. What if he *pretended* he didn't know to throw us off his trail?"

"It does seem odd to me that he didn't know," Piper said.

"Does he have a temper? Would he get money if Daniel died?"

Piper pieced together her interactions with Kristoff. He always worked in the background, doing things around the apartment for Daniel. He disappeared when she visited. "I don't know enough about him to say. I never saw a temper, but he was on duty when I saw him. Would he show a temper at work?"

Rosie bit her lip and grinned. "I do." Her laugh rang out and filled the car with the light sound.

"Good thing you work for your friend, huh?" Piper smiled, thankful for quirky Rosie. "Let's stop at the academy before home. I want to check if the cleaners came."

"Are you going to see if Trefor removed your piano?" Rosie asked.

A shiver ran through Piper, and her shoulders twitched. "No. I can't look."

"I'll check for you," Rosie said. "You find out if Lisa left a message on your office phone."

"Good idea." Piper nodded, a new sense of unease rolling in her stomach. She knew Lisa hadn't just dropped off the face of the earth.

"Change of plans. I'd rather stop at the bookstore first and see what Becky's heard today," Piper said as they drove through downtown Cranberry Harbor. Piper scanned the sidewalks looking for the culprit. *Come on, Piper—you're losing it. A murderer isn't going to walk downtown carrying a sign.*

"Good idea," Rosie said. "But can we stop at Sweetberry's first? I need a muffin." She turned a pouting face toward Piper. "Please," she whined.

Piper pulled into the lot at Sweetberry's. "Make it quick and get me a brownie."

"Aye aye, Captain." Rosie saluted.

Piper locked the door when Rosie hopped out of the car. Cranberry Harbor wasn't a lock-your-door type of town, but her frazzled nerves and shaky mind couldn't handle surprises. She didn't want to speak to anyone, so she scooted down in the seat and closed her eyes.

Piper jumped at the knock on her window, her heart pounding.

"Open the door, Piper!" Rosie stood outside the car, frowning. "You worried the boogey man's gonna get ya?"

"Well, Rosie, things are rather odd around town—you never know." She took a bite of brownie, "Mmm . . . oh my—this is delicious."

Rosie smiled and raised her muffin. "Cheers. I don't know how you eat so much chocolate, Piper. Makes my teeth hurt."

"I don't know how you *don't* eat chocolate, Rosie. This brownie is going straight to my hips, but I don't care today. Anyone say anything in there?"

"Nothing other than Dominique said Lisa didn't stop in for her muffin this morning."

"What's going on? That's not like her. She stops at Sweetberry's every morning." A heaviness settled in Piper's heart. "We need to check on her."

"Bookstore first, but I'll write this clue in the notebook quick." Rosie took a bite of her muffin and pointed down the street. "Onward, my friend."

Kindred Spirits Book Shoppe was the last store at the end of Main Street—right before Glacier Lake. A family hurried down the pathway to the beach, lugging bags and toys. The little boy yelled, "I wanna go to the bookstore!"

"Later," his mom said.

Piper glanced at the family for a moment. If the lake weren't so cold, she would take a swim to ease her mind and rest her brain. Less than twenty-four hours into this awful situation, she couldn't shake her exhaustion. Her tight shoulders and the pit in her stomach hurt. Her tired mind churned memories and clues like the rock tumbler she played with years ago churned pebbles and rocks. Everything bounced around, and nothing made sense—she followed Rosie inside the store.

The tinkling of the bells above the door and the unique scent of old books filled the store. Rosie leaned on the counter, speaking to an employee. Piper glanced around the store for the owner—her friend Becky.

"Piper!" Becky called, wiping her hands on her shirt. "That book on Debussy came in. I'll grab it for you, but I didn't expect you to come in so soon after . . ." Becky stopped and bit her lip.

Piper smiled a tight smile. "I forgot about the Debussy book, but thank you; I'll pay my bill now. Rosie and I wondered if we could ask you a few questions."

"Follow me." Becky led Piper to an area in the back of the store, their footsteps echoing on the hardwood floor. Tables and chairs arranged on a plush rug offered a spot to sit and peruse books or study—empty today.

"What do you need? A hug?" Becky wrapped her arms around Piper, patting her back for several moments. "I can't even imagine. How are you?"

Piper felt the dam of emotion breaking and bit her tongue to hold back tears. A lone tear escaped, and she wiped it away as Rosie bopped into the space.

"There you are. Thought I lost you for a minute." Rosie dropped into one of the chairs and pulled out the notebook.

"What have you heard today, Becky? Anything odd or out of place? Anyone acting strange?" Piper asked.

Becky frowned. "Nothing. Nothing that I can nail down. Business seems normal for a summer day, and I haven't overheard anything odd. Everyone's discussing the news and wondering what happened. It's awful and so unexpected in Cranberry Harbor."

Piper and Rosie nodded.

"Who came in today?" Rosie asked.

Becky listed several regular customers and mentioned the usual tourist traffic. "Lisa called yesterday and said she'd pick up her book order first thing this morning, but she never came in."

"What book?" Piper asked.

Becky stood. "Follow me—I'll grab it." She pulled out a bag from under the counter and handed it to Piper.

Piper pulled the book from the bag and dropped it onto the counter with a scowl. "Why did Lisa order a book called *How to Hide a Body*? When did she order this?"

Becky pulled up the record on her computer. "Three days ago. In her defense, it's a novel, not a how-to manual."

"Please tell me there's nothing in here suggesting piano crates?" Piper rubbed her temples.

"I haven't read it, so I can't say. But Lisa hasn't read it either," Becky said.

"Good point." Rosie scribbled in the notebook and said, "Piper, you should pay for the book and force Lisa to explain when we find her."

"Excellent idea," Piper said, handing Becky her credit card. "Add the Debussy book too. Any other chatter you've heard?"

"Mrs. Schmidt says you're doing this for some marketing ploy—to create buzz for the academy."

Piper stared at her friend. "Are you kidding me? Who in their right mind could think I *wanted* this to happen?"

Becky blinked. "Well, if you intended to use it for marketing, it worked. No one can stop talking about your music academy."

"My academy will fold if I don't clear my name. Who'd send their kids to a murderous piano teacher?"

"You're a suspect?" Becky asked.

"Not yet. But I'm not sitting around waiting for the police to name me. Rosie and I will figure out who did this and get my life and academy back to normal."

"Good luck, kindred spirits!" Becky called as Piper and Rosie hurried out.

"We don't need luck—we need prayer," Piper replied. "Will you call the prayer chain for me? Ask them to pray for a quick end to this tragedy and for wisdom."

"You got it." Becky rested her hands together as if she were praying.

"Thank you!" Piper called and shut the front door. The cheerful bells tinkled overhead.

"Who should we interview next?" Piper asked. She adjusted the volume on the radio and backed out of the parking spot at the bookstore. "My brain can't remember who else is on the list."

Rosie opened the notebook and read from the list. "Felicity Graves."

Piper groaned. "Too soon, plus I need a good night's sleep before facing Daniel's widow. Want to go in the morning?"

Rosie nodded and read the list. "Daniel's secretary—check. Chase, Braden, your parents, and Lisa? We're writing Lisa down now, correct?"

Piper nodded. "What are we missing? There has to be someone we aren't thinking of."

"I don't know, Piper." Rosie sighed. "I've never solved a murder before, and I'm exhausted. What if we skip stopping at the academy, get some sleep, and start fresh in the morning?"

Piper glanced at her watch. "You're right. It's almost time for supper, and no one wants to talk this late. Plus, I need to break it to my dad that I'm staying at my house."

Rosie whistled. "Getting brave in your old age, huh? Didn't The Core decide you would stay with your parents?"

"Yes, they did, and how did you know that?"

Rosie's eyes sparkled. "I have my ways." She laughed and clapped her hands, her bracelets jingling.

Piper's gritty eyes begged for sleep, and Rosie was right—time to call it a night and get rest. "Our brains can sort the pieces out while we sleep."

"You can hope," Rosie said. "Want to drive past the academy?"

Piper yawned. "Too tired. Can you write the academy on our list for tomorrow? You'll go inside with me, right?"

"Of course, but aren't you supposed to take Lenny with you?"

Piper rolled her eyes and sighed. "We'll survive without taking him."

"Is that your mom?" Rosie pointed to a woman entering The Wooly Llama Yarn Store.

"I think so—that's her favorite shop."

"How does she have time to knit?"

"Who knows? How do *you* have time to *paint*?"

"Painting is my life," Rosie said. "I always have time."

"Should we pop in and see if Cassidy's heard any good buzz today?"

"I'm sure she has, but I have to get home. I'm about to fall asleep." Piper turned off the main road and headed for her neighborhood. She dreamed of a hot bath and a cup of tea with something chocolate.

She turned into her Ferry Crossing neighborhood—reporters and news vans lined the street. "Oh, man," Rosie sighed. "Want me to drive, and you can slouch down in the back seat?"

"No, I'm driving straight through and ignoring everything." Piper stiffened her spine and stared ahead.

She navigated the busy road and pulled into her driveway. She and Rosie dashed to the back door as reporters shouted questions from the street. Piper's hand trembled when she inserted the key into the lock. The women hurried inside and dropped onto Piper's kitchen stools.

"This is crazy, Piper. I don't think you should stay here. What if one of those crazies breaks in or goes through your trash?" Rosie asked.

Piper waved her hand and stood to brew tea. "I'm fine. I'll check messages and emails, take a hot bath, and head straight to my bed."

"And call your dad."

"Yes," Piper sighed. "Let my dad know I'm not obeying orders." She rolled her eyes. "That should go over well."

Rosie hugged Piper and gave her a quick kiss on the cheek. "I love you, friend. Be safe."

"You too," Piper said, locking the door behind Rosie.

Her phone rang. "Lenny?"

"Where are you, Piper?"

"At my house. Why?"

Lenny sighed. "Piper, I thought The Core decided you would stay with your parents."

"I can't, Lenny. I need my bed and my office."

"Did you tell your father?"

"No. Will you, please?"

Lenny sighed again. "Sure. Make Lenny do the dirty work."

"Why did you call?"

"Chief Maxwell called. He said he wants to talk to you tomorrow morning at nine, but no new info today. I'll let him know you're at your home."

"No new information? Cause of death? Suspects?"

"They aren't going to tell us any of that while investigating. I'll keep after him and let you know when I hear anything."

"Thanks, Lenny."

"Listen, Piper—you need to stay safe. I'll tell your dad you're at your house, but you need to lock up. Don't answer the door unless you know who's on the other side or know they're coming over. Close your curtains and bring your trash to your parent's. Do not throw anything away outside at your place. Got it?"

"Yes, sir."

"Get done whatever you think you need to do over there because I feel your father will drive over to collect you the minute he finds out."

"Wait to tell him for a while then, Lenny. I'm a big girl."

"Yes, but we're talking about a murder here, and we have no idea who did this and why they dumped the body in your piano."

"I promise I'll do everything in my power to stay safe."

Piper checked her window locks and closed the curtains. She loved the old house she had bought on a whim. She had driven past the painted lady every morning for years and admired the turret. The wide porch surrounding the whole house was a major selling point for Piper. Victorian-style architecture made her smile, and this house was a perfect specimen. When she saw the "For Sale" sign on her way to work one morning, she pulled over, wrote the realtor's name down—and signed the papers the next day.

"I know you needed me to spend the Steinway money on you, you poor old house," she said while she locked doors and closed windows. "But I needed the new piano for the academy. I'll get you fixed up. I promise." She patted the stair rail on her way upstairs. The wood worn smooth by countless hands of people who had held the railing on their way up or down these stairs made Piper smile. She imagined other people who lived and loved here. "I know I'm crazy for talking to you, but I'm glad you're my house, old friend," Piper said. She shut her bedroom door and sunk into the soft mattress. "I'll rest for a minute—then the emails," she whispered and fell asleep.

CHAPTER THREE

Thursday

A faint knocking woke Piper. *I'm so tired that I'm hearing things.* She rolled over and burrowed deep underneath her blankets. When her alarm played Debussy's "Mandoline," Piper rolled over to grab the phone, and her hand brushed against a cold, hard object. It crashed to the floor with a clatter. The knocking grew louder, and Piper hopped out of bed and screamed when pain shot through her foot.

"Owww . . ." She hopped a couple of tiny steps and glanced at a pile of green glass shards. When she bent to examine the glass, a frog face lay on the floor staring at her. She frowned. "Where did this come from? Where are all these frogs coming from?"

The knock shook her front door. Piper jerked open her bedroom door and yelled, "I'm coming!"

Who in the world is knocking at my door at this hour? I can't believe I fell asleep in my clothes.

She patted her hair and retied the Van Gogh scarf around her neck.

I don't know how I fell asleep wearing this scarf.

The knock at the door escalated into banging. "I'm coming!" Piper yelled and bit back the angry words on her tongue. "If that's you, Roosevelt, so help me . . ."

She held her foot off the floor and tried to keep the blood from dripping onto her carpet. She slammed open the heavy front door. "Why can't you call like a normal person?"

Chief Maxwell stood on the porch, frowning. He nodded to her foot. "Do you need a bandage, Miss Haydn?"

She sighed. *Yep, dripping blood everywhere.* "Yes, apparently I do."

"Sit down. Where are they?" he asked.

Piper pointed up. "Bathroom cabinet—top of the stairs."

Chief Maxwell came down with a towel and bandages. "What happened here?" He knelt and wrapped the towel around her foot.

"I knocked things off my nightstand when I woke up. When I jumped out of bed to see who was banging at my door, I stepped on the pieces."

"Sorry," he said, dabbing her foot and reaching for a bandage. "I did tell your attorney I'd be over at nine."

She grabbed her phone. *Ten after nine already? How did I sleep that long?*

"He told me. I guess I hit snooze too many times without checking the time."

Chief Maxwell pointed at her scarf. "But you dressed?"

"Fell asleep like this."

He nodded. "I get that. Murder is stressful."

She gazed at him, grateful for his help, but why did he seem human today—so kind—not all business?

He's trying to butter me up so I'll spill my guts. Well, Chief Maxwell, there's no guts to spill. I didn't murder my ex.

"Why did you need to talk to me?" she asked.

He grunted when he stood. "I wanted to ask you if your accountant has gone through your financials recently."

She frowned. "My assistant Lisa handles that for me. Why?"

"Did you have any discrepancies in your accounting? Missing money? Too much money? Anything off?"

"No. Everything's in order. I've requested this month's printout from Lisa and will let you know if I see something amiss."

"You do that. How about you call me when she gets the paperwork to you?"

"Yes, sir."

"Reporters bothering you? I can send them farther down the street if you wish."

"No," Piper said. "They shout questions when I drive in or out, but no one's come on my property yet."

"I thought you were staying with your parents." He frowned.

"I'm a big girl, Chief Maxwell."

He smiled and his eyes twinkled.

What does that mean?

He turned away to cough, and heat rose in Piper's cheeks.

What in the world? Is he flirting with me?

"Is that all, sir?" She spoke in her professional music teacher voice—the voice her students obeyed.

"Yes, Miss Haydn. That's all for right now. When I have more information or have questions, I'll get in touch with you."

He had almost reached his cruiser when Piper remembered her question.

"Chief Maxwell," she called from the door. "Is my academy released?"

He nodded. "They picked up the piano this morning. Do you have a cleaning crew coming?"

Piper nodded. "As soon as you release the building, I'll call."

"Go ahead then. Stay safe."

Piper shut the door, twisted the lock, and rubbed her eyes. She limped to the kitchen to brew coffee and yawned. *I'll check all the emails and messages I missed when I zonked out last night. But first—coffee!*

The notebook and book she had purchased at Kindred Spirits lay on the counter where she dropped them last night. She pushed the investigation notebook aside and flipped through the book on Debussy. Piper filled a mug with coffee and made her way to her sitting room in the turret. She enjoyed drinking coffee on the large porch when Wisconsin's weather cooperated, but the hovering reporters made relaxing on the porch impossible this morning.

Piper settled into a chair and sighed when she pulled out her phone—so many messages.

---**Hey, Trefor here. Can I bring coffee?**

----**Yes, please, another large latte from Ruby's if you don't mind.**

She smiled at his kind text. *Maybe I should give him another chance.*

He always behaved like a perfect gentleman, and he was attentive to her needs. But his personality often rubbed her the wrong way—he was fine for a friend, but he wasn't the man of her dreams. She grabbed her phone and found several messages from Rosie.

--**What time should I come over?**

--**You up?**

--**On my way. Stopping at Sweetberry's. Bringing chocolate.**

Rosie knew her too well. She appeared flighty and lost in her creative world much of the time, but Piper loved her childhood friend. Rosie's friendship and loyalty were priceless. "Thank you, God, for Rosie. And please, God, help us figure this out." She whispered a prayer before turning back to her phone.

She scrolled for several minutes, answering the messages she could respond to quickly. Several employees texted, wondering when the academy would open for business. Several parents sent messages of concern and asked when lessons would resume.

She answered most of the parent messages with a copy and paste,

--**Thank you for your concern. The police released the academy this morning. After we clean, I will send out**

an announcement on continuing lessons and classes. I appreciate your patience.

She had opened her emails to determine what fires needed extinguishing when her phone rang. She groaned and turned on her chipper voice. "Morning, Daddy."

"Morning yourself, Piper Grace Haydn. Did we or did we not decide at The Core meeting that you would sleep at the house?"

"I did, Daddy," she said in a fake innocent voice.

"You know what I mean, Piper. I woke up this morning and discovered you disobeyed. Good grief, child—I'm trying to keep you safe."

"Daddy, I'm not a child, and I needed to rest in my bed. Please don't be angry. I fell asleep before it got dark and slept all night. I'm ready to tackle the day—not exhausted and worried. I need my own space."

Her father sighed on the other end of the line. "I know you're grown up, but this isn't a small thing we're trying to navigate. You're not talking to reporters, are you?"

"Of course not, Daddy," she said. "I'm offended. You know me better than that."

"They're circling, trying to find a big scoop. It's the biggest news event in Cranberry Harbor in decades. If I had realized Daniel Graves would cause so much trouble, I would have wrung his neck months ago."

"Daddy, you can't say that."

"I *will* say it. Daniel added nothing to our lives—or yours. I wish you'd never laid eyes on the man."

"I agree, but it's too late. Please, if I had the chance to change anything about that history, I would. I'm sorry the murder is disturbing your business. How's the orchard?" she asked, changing the subject.

"Busy. Apples are doing well, and cherries are progressing. Robert tells me he expects a bumper crop this year. Enough about that—you stay safe. I don't want to hear that you and Roosevelt are getting in the way of the investigation or that you're doing something dangerous."

"Daddy, come on."

"I know you two. I'm serious." His voice dropped. "I love you, Piper Grace. I can't stand thinking about the awful things that might happen to you."

"Don't, Daddy. Trust the Lord, right? Isn't that what you always tell me?"

He laughed and said, "Don't you preach at me. Those are my words."

"Well, they're good words. We'll trust the Lord together. Oh, someone's at the door—gotta go."

She hung up and limped to the front door. Rosie and Trefor stood outside, their hands full.

Piper opened the door and motioned them in while reporters shouted from the road.

She slammed the door and reached for the coffee, taking a big sip. "Thank you both. You're lifesavers."

"Can I wash up?" Trefor asked.

Piper pointed to the kitchen and settled into a chair in the sitting room. She sank her teeth into the brownie and groaned. "Dominique bakes the best brownies. I have to quit eating these."

"Chocolate is good for your stress, so you say. You need two. What's up with him always needing to wash?" Rosie whispered.

Piper shrugged and whispered, "OCD?"

"I'll OCD *him*. You shoulda seen him glaring at me when we waited for you to open the door."

"That's 'cause you laughed at him about his girlfriend."

Rosie grinned. "It *is* a bit funny, Piper. You have to admit it."

Piper smiled, trying to stay diplomatic. "He's sad. Give him a break. Shh."

Trefor stepped into the room, "What happened to your foot?"

"Stepped on broken glass. Don't worry—I'm fine. Sit. Let's compare notes. Can you grab the notebook, Rosie? It's on the kitchen counter," she said, pointing to her bandaged foot.

Rosie hopped up and came back with a frown. "It's gone."

"What?" Piper stood up and hobbled to the kitchen. "I left the notebook sitting on the counter this morning. I pushed the stack of books out of my way when I made coffee, but the notebook was definitely right there." She pointed to the empty spot on her counter.

Trefor walked to the back door and jiggled the handle. "It's locked," he said. "Are you sure no one else came in?"

"Chief Maxwell stopped by before you came, but I don't remember him going to the kitchen." She frowned. "I guess I'm not sure where he was. He helped me bandage my foot. If he came in here to wash his hands, I didn't notice."

"Did you take the notebook to your room last night?" Rosie asked.

"No. I left it right here." Piper pointed to the counter. "At least I *think* I did. I don't know." She sighed and rubbed her eyes.

"If the police took your notebook without a warrant, I'd file a complaint," Trefor said, his hands on his hips. "That's not right. What was in the notebook anyway?"

"Our rambling thoughts about who we suspect. We can recreate it. Right, Rosie?"

Rosie nodded, her dangling earrings tinkling. "Of course. But I'm finishing my muffin first."

Piper followed her back to the sitting room and settled in the chair with her brownie and coffee. Sun shone through the windows and streamed over the piano. "Trefor, Chief Maxwell said Notes picked up the Steinway this morning."

Trefor leaned on the doorjamb, his hands in his pockets. His Hawaiian print button-up shirt was open, showing a tee underneath that said, "Crazy Cat Guy." He held his Yeti mug decorated with stickers from the national parks. "Yeah, my boss sent a truck. He's working out the details with Steinway and the store's insurance policy. He'll let you know what's going on when he knows."

She nodded. "Thank you. I can't stand seeing that piano again." She shuddered.

"Have you played? Since . . . ?" he asked.

Piper nodded. "At my parents' the other day. I pounded out some furious music 'til I felt better." She smiled a weak smile. "I've not played mine, though."

"You will—when you're ready," Rosie said, nibbling her muffin. She glanced out the window and growled. "When will the reporters go away and leave you alone?"

"When the news goes away, I guess." Piper chewed a bite of her brownie and checked her watch. "Trefor, don't you have your baby music class soon?"

He jumped away from the doorframe. "Yes—gotta run. See you later, ladies." He slung a bag over his shoulder and ran out the door. The reporters shouted when he walked out.

Piper and Rosie stared out the window. "Why's he talking to them?" Piper frowned.

Rosie knelt on the sofa to peer out the window and scowled. "Trefor, come on, man." She knocked on the window, but he ignored them.

A strange feeling tumbled through Piper's mind, but she couldn't force the threads and pieces of clues into words. "Hopefully, the reporters asked him something innocuous like where he works or why he's here," she said.

"Well, I don't approve. We all agreed we wouldn't talk to the media," Rosie said.

Piper smiled and patted Rosie's shoulder. "Thanks, friend."

"Should we recreate the notebook?" Rosie asked.

"No," Piper said. "Let's stop at the academy so I can check what type of cleaning crew I need to hire. Have you heard from Lisa yet?"

"Negative, boss," Rosie said.

"I'm worried about her. She should answer my texts at least. Right?"

"You'd think. But who knows? This whole thing has everyone spooked," Rosie said. "Let's get going, and then we're talking to Daniel's wife, right?"

Piper frowned. "She's the last person I want to see."

"We want to solve the mystery, right?"

"Yes, but I feel everyone thinks I did something wrong."

"Listen, Piper—we've been over this. You didn't know, and you did nothing wrong."

"I know, but I still feel gross," Piper said. "I should call Pastor and Mrs. James. If I counsel with them, they'll help me have clarity."

"Excellent idea. Call Pastor on the way. If we don't get moving, we'll never have enough time to talk to everyone and solve this mess." Rosie jumped up, licked her fingers, and wiped her hands on her paisley palazzo pants.

"Where did you find those beauties?" Piper asked.

Rosie did a twirl and said, "Guess."

"Don't tell me . . . Cranberry Closet?"

"Nope, not the thrift store this time—Granny's Treasures." Rose winked, "Aren't they amazing?"

"They're amazing on you. I'd look like a clown." Piper called on her way upstairs, "Let me change, and we can leave!"

Piper hurried down the stairs a few minutes later in a black pencil skirt, white polo shirt, and black ballerina flats. She tied her ponytail in a pale violet silk scarf.

Rosie eyed Piper from head to toe. "Well, at least your scarf isn't boring. One of these days I'll pizzazz you up, Piper Haydn. You need some spice in your life."

Piper grabbed her keys. "No way—this murder mystery is all I need. When it's over, I'm going back to boring Miss Haydn, and I'm going to enjoy it."

Rosie laughed and followed her to the car.

The academy was eerily quiet for a weekday. On a typical day, cars filled the parking lot, and the drop-off lane never emptied. On most days, moms chatted on the sidewalk, and classes of little ones practiced dancing on the enclosed playground. But today, Piper's car was the only one in the lot. Crime tape surrounded the building.

"Gives me the creeps," Rosie said and shivered. "Looks haunted."

"Ignore that feeling. We should check on how much of a mess was left behind and call the cleaning crew. I want to print the financials while I'm here, and you putter around Lisa's office and see if she left a calendar or a note. I don't remember her asking for time off, but who knows? My brain seems so muddled right now."

Piper opened the front doors and disabled the alarm but locked the door with a shudder. "I'm not leaving the door unlocked with the two of us alone here."

"Good idea." Rosie followed her through the academy, taking notes as Piper pointed out rooms and areas needing attention.

"I expected a worse mess. I shouldn't need to hire a big cleaning crew," Piper said.

Piper stood in the hallway outside the auditorium and gripped the door handle for several moments while her stomach churned. She breathed in and out to soothe her racing heart.

"You don't have to go in there," Rosie said.

"Oh, but I do. If I let myself off the hook today, I'll avoid the auditorium next time, and then whoever did this wins." Piper straightened her spine and took a deep breath. "I'm ready, Rosie."

Rosie held her fingers in the air and counted, "One, two, three . . ." Piper jerked open the door on three, and the girls hurried into the empty auditorium. Rosie flipped on the overhead lights, and they stared at the stage. Floodlights shone on the bare spot where the new Steinway belonged.

"I'll bring the old piano back in. That will draw attention away from the missing Steinway." She dropped into a seat and rubbed her eyes.

Rosie sat next to Piper and pulled her into a hug. "Let everything out, friend."

Piper cried a great big ugly cry, her chest heaved with the sobs, and her nose ran.

Rosie disappeared and came back with tissues and water. She sat next to Piper and patted her arm. "You all right now?"

Piper nodded, dabbing her red eyes. "I believe I cried about everything."

"Your whole life." Rosie smiled and nudged her.

Piper stood. "Glad that's over. Let's print the financials and see if Lisa left any info in the office. Then we can attempt a chat with Felicity Graves."

"Let's do it, friend," Rosie said. She skipped ahead of Piper down the hall, singing a song Piper didn't recognize.

"You're not defiling the halls of my academy with country music, are you, Roosevelt Hale?" Piper called.

"Yes, I am, and you can't stop me!" Rosie turned and stuck her tongue out at Piper.

Piper giggled. "Good thing I like you."

Rosie's soft laugh echoed down the hall, and Piper smiled.

What would I do without Rosie?

"I can hear your thoughts, Piper Haydn. You can't survive without me. You'd die of boredom."

"Something like that." Piper laughed.

Rosie stuck her head out of the office. "The police left a mess in here, boss."

Piper sighed. Every single thing in her life was a mess—even her well-ordered work space.

We'll fix this. Right, God? Please.

She took a deep breath and braced herself before entering her office.

Piper sorted papers and tossed trash into the waste bin. Her mind churned, trying to slide the puzzle pieces together.

Who did this? Why? What did they want?

She rubbed her temples. "Rosie, are you finding anything on Lisa's desk or in her files?"

"No, her desk is in order. Did she ask you for days off?"

"I can't remember. We need to swing by her house when we leave. Will you open her computer and print out the last six months of accounting documents? I'll look over them tonight. Chief Maxwell wanted me to double-check if I found anything out of place."

"I'll look through her calendar too!" Rosie called from the outer office.

Piper pushed back from her desk and straightened piles of paper. She grabbed the porcelain frog. "Rosie, do you have any idea where these frogs are coming from?"

Rosie frowned. "No. Why?"

"I keep finding little green frogs around. That's what I stepped on when I got out of bed this morning."

Rosie tapped her lips and frowned. "So odd."

Piper set the frog on her desk and grabbed her purse. "Let's swing by Lisa's and see what's going on." She grabbed the documents and hurried into the hall. The empty academy's quiet corridors raised goosebumps on her arms, and she ran to the door.

"Wait up!" Rosie called. "What was that?"

Piper glanced behind her at the dark building. "I don't know. Something gave me the creeps for a minute there. Like someone was watching us."

Rosie smiled and hugged Piper. "I'm sorry. Anyone would feel that way after all of this mayhem. The situation is hard for everyone. But look—the sun is shining. Nothing to fear."

"You're right. My imagination got the better of me. Let's go. You drive." Piper tossed the keys to Rosie and smiled.

The drive to Lisa's house took less than five minutes along the lakeshore. Piper took a deep breath and tried to settle her mind.

There's an explanation for all this—why they involved my academy. What is it?

Rosie parked at the curb in front of Lisa's modest brick home on the edge of town. Her lawn was overgrown, and the flowers needed a big drink of water. The house looked a little unloved.

Piper knocked, and they waited on the porch holding their breath. After several knocks, Piper turned back to the car.

"What do you think of that?" Rosie asked.

Piper frowned. "I don't like it. Lisa didn't say she needed time off or tell me she'd be gone. She's not answering her phone or text messages. What are your thoughts?"

Rosie glanced at the windows, and Piper shifted to peek at Lisa's house. The home appeared vacant, but a curtain fluttered in an upstairs window.

"Did you see that?" Piper pointed.

"Yep. That curtain moved."

Piper picked up her phone, punched in Lisa's number, and got the voicemail. "Lisa, we're getting very worried about you. I'm at your house, and you didn't answer, but we see a curtain moving. Are you safe? Please? I don't want to worry about anyone else right now. Call me back."

Rosie frowned. "I don't know if that was anybody. Look close—the window is open. Probably the wind."

"I feel uneasy about this," Piper said. "Should I tell someone at the police department?"

"Maybe. Where to next?"

"Daniel's wife, I guess." Piper took a deep breath and closed her eyes.

"I can take you home and pick up Trefor. He and I can question her. You should go home and decompress. Comb through the accounting documents while we question people. I can't do the accounting for you anyway," Rosie said.

"No, I have to do this." Piper smiled a tight smile and sighed.

Rosie parked at the end of the drive and whistled. "There's a McMansion if I ever saw one," she said, peering through the windshield. "At least we brought your car. Mine would look out of place here."

"If this is a McMansion, what's my parent's house?" Piper asked.

"Your parents are *actually* rich, not trying to *pretend* they're rich. Your house is your house. Classy. This thing is a monstrosity." Rosie pulled the keys out of the ignition. "Ready?"

Piper took a deep breath and nodded. The doorbell chimed and echoed.

Please don't be home. Please don't be home. She laid a hand on her knotted stomach and tried to calm her breathing.

"No one's home. Let's go," Piper said and turned to the car.

Rosie grabbed her hand. "Shh—I hear footsteps." The door opened, and Piper caught her first glimpse of Felicity Graves. Daniel's wife stood inside the door, staring at them, her eyebrows raised. Dressed in a long black cardigan, lace top, and skinny jeans, she looked younger than her forty-five years.

"Mrs. Graves," Piper said. "We're sorry to—"

"Felicity," she said, interrupting.

Piper frowned.

"You said, 'Mrs. Graves,' and I said, 'Felicity.' Don't call me 'Mrs. Graves.'"

"I'm sorry. We're sorry to bother you, but we have a couple of questions."

"A couple of questions for the grieving widow?" She rolled her eyes. "I know who you are." She pointed at Piper.

Piper's cheeks flushed, and she stepped back, "I . . . umm . . . how?"

The woman gave a mirthless laugh, her voice gruff and husky—a cigarette smoker. "Oh, I know all about Daniel's exploits, his apartment, and that creepy secretary who does his dirty work. I've known about you for months, Piper," she said, spitting out Piper's name.

Piper shivered. "Well, I didn't know about *you.*"

Felicity Graves laughed again, and the sound grated Piper's nerves. "You should have kept him, you know. Not sure why he jilted you at the altar. I didn't want him."

"Wait." Rosie stuck her foot inside the door as Felicity stepped away.

Felicity raised her eyebrows and stared at Rosie's foot. "What do you think you're doing? Get off my property before I call the cops. That will sound nice in the papers, huh, Miss Haydn?" She sneered. "'Dead man's floozy attempts entry into grieving widow's home.' I'm sure your daddy would love the press."

She stepped back into the house, and Rosie blurted, "Did you kill him?"

Felicity stared a moment, and her laugh erupted in a blast. She held her side and wiped her eyes. "Oh, oh—that's funny. Did I kill Daniel? No. No, I did not kill my *husband.*" She emphasized *husband.* "But I should have after everything he did to me. The embarrassment, the whispers, the deception. Maybe I should have killed him for all the diseases he brought home to me." She raised her eyebrow and pointed at Piper. "You might want to get yourself checked, hon. He was a disgusting man." She turned back to Rosie and jabbed a finger in her direction. "No. I didn't kill Daniel, but whoever did it did me a favor, and when I find out, I'm going to say thanks. I'll have a drink with them while I dance on Daniel's grave. Now get out of here." She slammed the door.

Piper turned to Rosie, her eyes wide, and shivered as a chill passed through her. "What was *that*?"

Rosie hurried to the car. "I don't know, but I'd say the widow isn't grief-stricken."

Piper sank into the passenger seat. "Goodness—I've never felt so cold in my life. I didn't expect that. She's so beautiful, but . . ."

"Yeah, well, you know things aren't always how they appear, Piper."

Piper choked back a sob. "I can't wrap my mind around being happy he's gone when he just died. What if she paid someone?"

Rosie grimaced. "I don't know. It's possible. Might explain why she dumped his body at your academy if she knew about you."

Piper covered her face and whispered. "I don't understand hating someone so much that you'd kill them. I don't understand why someone would bring that horror to my academy. I . . ." She covered her mouth.

"Are you sick?" Rosie shrieked and pulled the car to the side of the road. Piper hopped out, her stomach heaving and twisting.

She climbed back into the car, and tears rolled down her cheeks. "I hate this."

Rosie patted her leg. "I hate this for you, and I'm sorry. Let's get you home and in bed for a bit."

Piper nodded and rested her head on the car window. Visions of Daniel's lifeless face and the sound of Felicity's rough laughter echoed in her mind.

God, what am I going to do?

Piper sat up and rubbed her temples. "Rosie, stop at Tea Thyme before you take me home. I want to ask Maisy what she's heard."

"Perfect. I want to try the new lavender tea and today is crème brûlée scone day." Rosie blew Piper a kiss. "Thanks for the suggestion."

Tea Thyme was across the street from the Kindred Spirits Book Shoppe. The violet striped awning stretched over the sidewalk, shading pots of flowers. A wicker bench with purple pillows sat under the front window, an inviting spot to rest and enjoy the scenery. Rosie plopped onto the bench and took a deep breath. "Perfect view." She patted the bench, and Piper perched on the edge and glanced around Main Street.

"Everything here is a perfect view," Piper said. "Glacier Lake, the harbor, the town." She frowned. "Rosie, I don't understand." She closed her eyes and leaned back on the bench. "Who did this?"

Rosie patted her leg. "I have no idea, but let's grab that tea before you sink into the depths of despair."

A bell over the door chimed when Rosie tugged at the door. Spices, tea, and herbs mixed into a heady fragrance, and Piper took a deep breath. "My goodness—no wonder Dad loves stopping here."

"Piper." The woman behind the counter sat down a teapot and wiped her hands on a purple gingham apron. She frowned. "How are you?"

"As good as you'd expect if you found a body in your new Steinway," Piper said.

Maisy frowned again and clucked her tongue. "It's so terrible, Piper. What is happening in this town? Who would do something so horrible?"

"I don't know, but Rosie and I are trying to find out. What have you heard? Any interesting theories?"

Maisy gasped. "Piper, are you supposed to be figuring this out? What did the police say?"

"That new chief told us to stay out of the investigation, but we can't," Rosie said. "This is Piper's life we're talking about here. We can't sit around and wait."

"No, no—I agree. I'm worried for you, though. I don't know of anyone capable of doing something so awful, but I don't need to worry that someone will come after *you*." Maisy stepped behind the counter and grabbed the teapot. "I'll boil water. What kind of tea should I brew? Something calming, Piper?" she asked.

Piper pinched the top of her nose and blew out a sigh. "Yes, please, something that will stop the shaking inside my body."

Maisy pouted. "You poor thing. I'll brew you some lemon balm. It gives you a little zap of energy, but it calms anxiety and nerves." Maisy handed her a bag. "Here—try this damask rose petal tea before bed. It will send you off to dreamland and help you stay asleep."

Piper smiled. "Thank you, Maisy."

"So what's the buzz, Maisy?" Rosie asked.

Maisy glanced out to the street and around the store. She leaned over the counter and whispered, "I'm not sure about this, so don't repeat it. But Ruby, Becky, and I got together to talk this morning before we opened. Sorry we didn't invite you. We didn't want to worry you, but . . ."

Piper's eyes widened. "But what?"

"All three of us have a weird feeling we can't explain, but we feel someone lurking around in the shadows watching. I haven't noticed anything off, but Ruby and Becky said they've seen some people hanging around who don't look like tourists." Maisy handed a steaming mug of tea across the counter to Piper.

Rosie scowled. "That doesn't help, Maisy. There are always tourists and new people around. We're a destination town."

"I know," Maisy said "I told the others that, but it's a feeling I can't shake, and neither can they."

"Have you seen someone hanging around or acting odd?" Piper asked.

Maisy frowned. "As I said, it's nothing I can explain, but we're keeping our eyes open. We'll tell you if we notice anything. But last night when I locked up, I got the distinct feeling someone was watching me."

Piper shivered. "I felt that way at the academy this morning. Right, Rosie?"

Rosie nodded, and her hoop earrings jingled. "When you ran to the front door? Yeah. I kinda felt it too."

Piper sank onto the stool at the counter and sipped tea. She grabbed a honey packet and stirred. "Maisy, who did this? It's so awful."

Maisy wiped the counter. "I don't know, Piper, but we have to figure it out. Is your dad upset about the publicity? It seems like he's protective of the Haydn reputation."

"Oh, yes—we've already held a meeting of The Core, and Dad told me to stay at their house."

"But you didn't listen, did you?" Maisy stood with her hands on her hips and stared at Piper.

Piper sipped, and her mind relaxed as the hot tea worked its magic. "I'm a big girl, Maisy. I needed my bed and space to sort out my emotions."

"Well, I want you to stay safe."

Rosie interrupted—"I need a lavender tea and six scones to go."

"We'll take twelve, Maisy. I'm going to eat my way through this mess." Piper sighed. "I'll have to take up marathon running if we don't solve this soon."

Maisy smiled. "Coming right up."

Rosie clutched the box of scones in one hand and her to-go cup of lavender tea. "Where to, boss?" She asked.

"My house, I guess. But drive around the business district first. Let's see if we see anyone or get a feeling like the girls did."

Rosie drove through the downtown area while Piper scanned the sidewalks and commented on people coming and going from shops. "I don't see anything off. Looks like a normal day to me."

"Should I head home then?" Rosie asked.

Piper nodded, and Rosie turned the car around. "Is that Lisa's car?" she asked, pointing down a side street.

Piper sat up and stared. "Not sure. Drive past."

"No, Lisa has those chicken and goat bumper stickers on her car," Rosie said. "I'm seeing things."

Piper sighed. "We all are. Head home. I'll warm up that pasta, and we can take notes."

"Deal, boss," Rosie said.

"Looks like a few reporters went home," Piper said when Rosie pulled into her driveway.

"About time."

From the remaining reporters came questions: "Piper, have the police given you any information? Miss Haydn, is it true that . . ."

Piper and Rosie hurried around to her back door to shield themselves from the yelling. "I wish they'd leave you alone, Piper. I don't want them hanging around out there bothering you."

Rosie popped her head around the side of the house. "Leave her alone, you vultures!" she yelled.

Piper grabbed Rosie's sleeve and pulled her through the back door. "Rosie, we agreed we wouldn't talk to them."

"I know, but I'm so mad."

"Well, I'm mad too, but they're doing their jobs."

"They need a life," Rosie said. "I need to run home for a bit. Will you be safe by yourself?"

"I'm a big girl, Rosie. I'm fine. But when you get back, let's go over to the music store and see what they say. And we need to write notes from our stops. I have no idea where that notebook went."

"Deal. Give me an hour." She kissed Piper on the cheek and breezed through the door.

Piper sighed and sipped the last of her tea. She jumped at a knock at the back door. "Rosie?"

Rosie stood on the porch pantomiming.

Piper scowled, "What?"

"Lock the door." Rosie mouthed, pointing down at the handle.

Piper locked the door. "I'm a big girl, Roosevelt Hale." She rolled her eyes.

Piper sank into the sofa in her turret sitting room and grabbed the financial documents and a highlighter. She sighed and glanced around her comfortable room. Her home gave her peace, but nothing had soothed her frazzled nerves these past couple of days.

Piper glanced at the documents. "I can't concentrate." Blowing out a frustrated breath, she moved to the piano and sat on the edge of the bench, stretched her fingers, and poured her frustration onto the keys. She pounded through Berlioz's "Symphony Fantastique" and rested for a moment until her breathing calmed. Piper played until anxiety drained from her body. She stopped playing and tapped high C several times, frowning at the odd twang. *Time to call the tuner.* She rested her hands on the keys, enjoying the cool, smooth surface of the piano keys. Patting the keyboard, she whispered, "Thank you."

"Okay—I can handle this project now." She grabbed the yellow highlighter and got to work.

An hour later, Piper's eyes glazed over. "And this is why I hire someone to do the accounting for me." She dropped the papers on the cushion next to her. So far, nothing odd stood out. She rubbed her eyes and stretched, glancing out the window at a loud noise at the end of her driveway. Rosie ran to the porch, and Piper hurried to the door.

She laughed and tugged Rosie inside, slamming the door. "It doesn't matter that my doorbell doesn't work. I know when someone's here by all the shouting out there." Piper rolled her eyes and took the coffee Rosie held out. "Perfect," she said and closed her eyes while the comforting scent of coffee relaxed her nerves.

Rosie pointed to the paper piles. "Anything?"

Piper sighed. "Nothing. I wish Lisa would pick up her phone and tell me what's going on. She can run through these figures in a few minutes. But it takes me hours, and I'm no closer to figuring out what's going on than when I started."

"Well, you know numbers are not my thing," Rosie said.

"They aren't mine either. That's why I pay Lisa." Piper grabbed her purse. "Ready to swing by the music store?"

"Aye, aye, captain." Rosie saluted Piper, and they snuck out the back door.

Rosie parked near the front door of Notes Music Centre. "Is Trefor still in class?" she asked as they hopped out of the car into the sunshine.

"I don't know. We can walk around the store if he's busy." Piper tugged open the door, and the sounds of a busy music studio poured out. Piano scales came from one end of the hall, and someone plucked notes on a guitar. Piper smiled and said, "Sounds like home."

"When will they let you open again?" Rosie asked.

"Depends on the cleaning crew. I need to decide today and get the information to the parents. If I restart classes soon, the academy can move past this without too much damage."

Rosie nodded and squeezed Piper's shoulders. "I hope so, Piper. You don't deserve any of this."

They walked toward Trefor's classroom and found him on the floor cross-legged, surrounded by ten cross-legged children. They sat, eyes closed, holding hands.

"What are they doing?" Rosie whispered, peeking through the big window. "He said 'music and movement class.' No one's moving."

Piper smiled. "Getting that many preschoolers to sit quietly is a marvel. Wonder what they're listening to."

A mother in the hallway said, "Feelings circle."

"Huh?" Rosie asked.

"It's a feelings circle. He closes every class with one to ground them. The children love him. He's a great teacher."

Piper nodded, and Rosie turned her back to the mom and rolled her eyes at Piper.

The children stood and bowed to Trefor, pretending to blow out a candle. Trefor waved at Piper when the last student left. "Piper, Rosie. Come in."

He waved them into the brightly decorated room. A keyboard and bins of instruments lined the wall. A round carpet printed with music notes sat in the middle of the room with large cushions around it.

"Wow—this is a nice setup!" Piper said. "Take notes, Rosie." She winked at Trefor.

"Imitation is the sincerest form of flattery, girls," Trefor said. "What brings you to Notes today? I planned to swing by your house and see if I could help tonight." He grabbed a bottle of strong hand sanitizer and rubbed the gel into his hands, and winced.

Piper rested her finger under her nose and cleared her throat. "What did you and the children do at the end of class?" Piper asked.

"Feelings circle?"

"Yes, what is it?"

"Oh, Piper—you've never done a feelings circle? I can't believe that. Sit down and let's try one. I bet your feelings are all over the board."

Piper smiled. "Not today, but explain how the circle works."

Trefor rested his hand on his chest and closed his eyes. "Oh, Piper, they are the best. We gather and light the candle—a battery-operated one 'cause they're preschoolers. Then I ring a bell. We sit still until the tones end. We go around the circle and share a weather word to share our current feelings."

"'Weather word'?" Rosie asked.

"You know, *stormy, sunny, cloudy.*"

Rosie nodded but rolled her eyes behind Trefor's back. Piper grinned and shot her a warning glance. They would giggle if Rosie didn't behave, and Piper knew Trefor was too sensitive to handle their laughter.

"We sit in silence for a few moments, and then I ask if anyone needs to add their log to the fire—their feelings. The children can move into the heat—or away from the circle if they're uncomfortable. We share a weather word for how they feel at the end. It's the best feeling in the world when they change their bad weather word for a positive one. I can't even explain. So much joy. Then they blow out the candle, I ring the bell, and they leave." Trefor sighed.

"How interesting!" Piper said.

"You should try it at the academy. Life-changing." Trefor closed his eyes and sighed again. "Let me clean up, and I'll show you around. Where did you want to tour?"

"Piano storage."

Trefor shivered. "Oh, Piper—you don't want to dredge up all those feelings."

"Those feelings are at the surface, Trefor. There's nothing to dredge up. I want to see."

He shrugged. "Up to you. Let's go."

Piper and Rosie hurried behind him down the hall to a large warehouse space. Several crates lined the wall and tools and piano wire hung from pegs. Piper glanced at the rows of pianos. "Tell me what happens here."

"Repairs and crating for delivery."

"So all the pianos here are waiting for a repair or delivery?" Piper asked.

"Most of them. Some are rehab projects for the sales floor, and a few pianos are for parts."

Piper nodded and walked around the space looking behind pianos and peering into dark corners. "Where was my Steinway?"

Trefor pointed to a far corner, and Piper hurried to the area. "Where does this hallway go?"

Trefor frowned. "Out to the big warehouse. Why?"

"It seems odd that there's an entrance close to where my piano sat. What if someone brought Daniel in that way?" She shivered.

Trefor's face paled. "Oh, Piper. I never thought of that." His hand shook, and he leaned against the wall. "I don't know. It's all so . . ."

"Awful." Rosie finished his sentence and fired questions at him. "Who knows about this entrance? Did the police investigate? Was her piano in the crate when it sat there?"

Trefor turned and walked away. "I have to get out of here."

Piper and Rosie followed him into the hall. He leaned on the wall and rubbed his forehead. "Piper, I wish I could take the sadness away from you. I'm sorry."

"Thanks, Trefor. We'll figure it out."

"Oh, hey." He stood up and smiled. "I have tickets for the Packers charity softball game Sunday. Can I pick you up around eight? We can tailgate."

Piper stared at Trefor. The sudden switch in topic left her unsettled. "I have church, Trefor." She frowned. "I loved them when I was younger, but I don't really follow the Packers anymore. Thanks, though."

Trefor said, "I bleed green and gold, Piper. Your loss. It's gonna be a great event. It raises money for kids."

Piper smiled. "Have fun. I need to get going now, but thanks so much for the tour."

"Thanks." Rosie waved and hurried behind Piper to the car and fell into the passenger seat laughing.

"What's so funny?"

"I don't know, but you should have seen his face when you said you don't do football. You know you're the odd one out around here."

"I know this entire state is full of crazed football fanatics, but I can't do it." She grimaced. "You should have told him you wanted to go."

Rosie laughed. "I'm a cheesehead with the best of them, but I'm not going anywhere with Trefor. He drives me nuts."

"You two are definitely oil and water." Piper smiled. "Let's drive by Lisa's again. I have to finish combing through that paperwork tonight, but I'm starving."

"I'll cook while you work," Rosie said.

"Um, no, Rosie. We'll order something."

Rosie's melodic laugh filled the car. "You're not hungry enough to deal with my cooking, huh?"

"I love you, Rosie, but no—I can't handle this murder and your cooking at the same time."

Rosie giggled. "I guess I'll have some stormy weather words to share with you when we hold the feelings circle tonight." Her bright laughter filled the car, and Piper took a deep breath.

Maybe everything will turn out fine.

Lisa's house sat dark and empty, and Piper's knock went unanswered. "This is getting strange, Rosie. Where is she?"

"Do you hear that?" Rosie asked.

Piper stood still for a moment and frowned. "Chickens?" They raced around the house and found Lisa's chickens pecking the dirt inside a coop.

"Do they look hungry?" Piper asked.

"How am I supposed to know what a hungry chicken looks like?" Rosie waved her hands in the air. "I'm not a farmer."

"Apparently, Lisa is. Did you know she has chickens and goats?" Piper pointed at a pen at the yard's edge holding three goats.

"Nope," Rosie said and tiptoed toward the goats. She squealed and jumped back when one bleated at her. Her eyes bugged out, and she patted her chest. "Oh, my goodness! Scared me half to death!" She laughed. "And don't ask me if they're hungry either. It's a regular farm around here."

"I can't imagine Lisa abandoning her animals. Something's wrong." Piper's heart raced, and she glanced around the yard. "I have the creeps again—let's get out of here."

Piper and Rosie hurried to the Mercedes, and Rosie clicked the locks shut. "I hate to say this, Piper, but I think Lisa has something to do with Daniel's murder."

"What? No way, Rosie. No. I can't believe that someone I work with every day is capable of this. No. She's worked hard for me for a long time and helped me grow and improve the academy with her ideas. I won't believe she murdered Daniel."

"It's a feeling I have. I know I never told you before, but I can't shake it. Lisa was furious when Daniel left you, and she ranted for weeks."

"We were *all* furious, Rosie. Me. My parents. My brothers."

"Me," Rosie whispered. "I wanted to strangle him with my bare hands."

"Well, see. My point exactly, and you better be careful about who's around when you say that. Chief Maxwell will haul you in."

"Speaking of the chief, did he call you today?"

"Not yet. He told me to comb through the financials before I called. I better get that done and give him a call." Piper glanced at her watch. "If I hurry I can catch him before the end of the workday."

"Get busy. I'll warm up dinner," Rosie said when they returned to Piper's house. She shooed Piper out of the kitchen. "No complaining—you know I'm ordering take-out." Her laugh followed Piper down the hallway.

Piper smiled and curled up on the couch with the financial reports and a highlighter. She scanned the lines of the printed ledger and whispered a prayer: "If there's something I'm supposed to see in these numbers, can you please help me, God? And help us figure out who did this. I'm so tired, and I want my life back."

She grabbed the first pile of papers and frowned. She flipped through the stack on the table, and her eyebrows furrowed. Piper grabbed the documents and limped to the kitchen, slowed by the cut on her foot.

"Rosie!" she called. "The fundraising money isn't in the accounts!"

"What?"

"The fundraising account isn't showing in any of the ledgers." Piper spread papers across the counter and pointed. "There's no mention of fundraising anywhere in these documents."

Rosie grabbed the sheets and scanned. "How much was in the account?"

Piper calculated figures in her mind. "I'm not even sure. The art fundraiser, the ongoing chocolate bar sale, the car wash."

"Don't forget the Christmas wreath sale," Rosie said. "When's the last time you spent money out of the account?"

"We haven't used fundraising money since last Christmas. I bought dance outfits and paid for a semester of lessons for three families. The account had thousands of dollars after I paid everything."

Rosie grimaced. "I told you I didn't want to accuse Lisa, but who else has access to the fundraising money besides you and her?"

Piper rested her head on her hands and sighed. "This is bad. What would cause her to take so much money? I never expected this—I trusted her."

"People do all sorts of things you don't expect. I don't know, but she doesn't look good, does she?"

Piper rubbed her eyes. "I'm exhausted from this chaos. I can't believe she took all this money—*and* murdered Daniel? I'm so confused."

"Did you hear how he died yet?"

"No, and I'm not sure I want to know."

"Let's write down our clues. You didn't find our missing notebook yet?"

Piper groaned. "We're striking out everywhere. I want off this crazy train."

"Me too. Oh, when I glanced through this Debussy book, I found something unusual." Rosie flipped through Piper's book from Kindred Spirits. "Guess what."

"Hmmm?"

"Debussy refused to compose unless his green porcelain frog sat on his desk."

Piper frowned. "What?"

"I know. Isn't that crazy? I guess all the composers had their quirks."

"No. I mean, that's odd. I keep finding glass frogs. I stepped on one and cut my foot."

"Oh, I didn't even think about that. Where are the frogs coming from?"

"I don't know, but there was one at my office. One on my nightstand."

"On your nightstand, Piper? That's creepy. Who has a key?" Rosie asked.

"Mom. You. The attorney."

"Your brothers? Lisa?"

"Yeah. Lots of people do."

"Is your mom dropping frogs off? Ask her," Rosie said. "But if we suspect Lisa and *she* has a key . . ."

"I will not accuse Lisa," Piper said. "I will ask Mom if she came in and left frogs for me, but I need to call Chief Maxwell first."

"He's kind of hunky." Rosie waggled her eyebrows at Piper.

Piper waved her off. "Oh, stop."

"What? I have eyes. He's definitely hunky."

Piper chuckled and grabbed her phone. "Find some paper, and we can take notes after I call."

When Piper opened the front door, she blushed. *He is hunky, Rosie. Why did you have to say that? Now I'm going to blush every time I see him.* Piper cleared her throat and stepped aside to let the officer inside. She glanced at his hand—no ring.

"Evening, Miss Haydn."

"Chief Maxwell, thank you for coming over. I went through the financials as you asked and didn't notice anything until my second time through. Our fundraising funds are missing." She handed the printouts to the chief.

"How much money are we talking about here?"

"I'm not positive, but there was ten thousand dollars the last time I used the funds."

"What's it used for, and who has access?" Chief Maxwell asked.

"The account is set aside for scholarships and helping underprivileged students. We also use the funds for upkeep or redecorating. My secretary, Lisa, and I are the only ones who can access the money."

"I haven't spoken with Lisa yet," Chief Maxwell said.

"Well, neither have we," Piper said.

He glanced up from the paperwork. "What do you mean?"

"Lisa doesn't answer my calls or texts, and when we stopped at her house, she didn't answer the door."

"We stopped twice," Rosie said. "And I think she killed Daniel."

Chief Maxwell stared at Rosie.

Piper said, "Rosie. Let's keep our theories to ourselves right now."

"Theories? Is that why you went to Felicity Graves's house today?" the chief asked.

Piper blushed. "I wanted to ask her a few questions."

Chief Maxwell snapped his notebook shut. "Leave the investigating to us. I mean it. Inserting yourself into a murder investigation isn't smart or safe. Do you understand?"

Piper and Rosie nodded.

"How's your foot, by the way?" he asked.

"Fine," Piper said.

"I'll check out your secretary's house and look at this ledger. Call the bank tomorrow and check if the account balance shows this money is missing, and call me."

"All right," Piper agreed.

"I mean what I said, ladies. You two stay out of this. I don't want anything happening to either of you on my watch."

When Piper shut the door behind Chief Maxwell, Rosie laughed. "I crossed my fingers when I promised."

Piper grinned. "Me too."

Piper sank onto the couch and rested her head. "Let's compare clues and take notes, Rosie. I need to sort the puzzle pieces."

Rosie grabbed a pen. " What should I write first?"

Piper rubbed her temples. "Felicity's happiness at Daniel's death."

Rosie nodded. "Can she afford to pay a hit man?"

Piper pursed her lips and stared across the room. "I imagine, but I don't know for sure. Their house seemed expensive."

"'Felicity hired a hitman.' I'll add a question mark. 'Lisa and the missing fundraising money.' What else?"

"The feeling that someone lurks around watching us."

Rosie laughed, and the cheerful sound settled over Piper, easing her stress. She smiled. "What?"

"Hey, hunky officer, we get the creeps around town. It's a clue." Rosie said.

Piper threw a pillow at Rosie. "Stop calling him 'hunky.' You're incorrigible."

Rosie raised her hands and tipped her head. "What? He *is* hunky, and he seems concerned about you. I didn't notice a wedding ring."

"Stop—back to the clues." Piper rolled her eyes.

"Kristoff," Rosie said.

Piper frowned. "Did you get any weird feelings from him? He acted shocked when you said Daniel died."

"I don't know. I never saw him before today, but, yes, Kristoff gave me the creeps."

"Is the creeps an official feeling?" Piper asked, and Rosie threw the pillow back. Piper ducked and giggled. "Murder is so stressful. Whoever imagined that we'd deal with such ugliness in Cranberry Harbor?" She closed her eyes.

Piper and Rosie jumped at a sudden pounding on the front door. "Dad?"

Jack Haydn stepped into the entryway and scanned the surrounding area. "Stopped in to check on you. What's going on? The chief left a message that you went to Daniel's house today. What are you thinking?"

"I'm sorting this out, Dad. I can't sit around waiting to get my life back."

"Listen, Piper Grace—that's why The Core decided you would stay at our house until this blows over."

"I'm a big girl, Daddy. I know you have feelings about Daniel, but this affects the academy and me. I need to figure everything out. The sooner we solve his murder, the sooner I get back to my students and my life."

"We aren't living in an episode of *Law & Order,* Piper Grace Haydn. This is real life, and some lunatic out there wanted to send you a terrible message. I don't want you mixed up in any danger."

"Too late, Daddy. Please don't worry about me. I take Rosie with me everywhere I go." Piper said.

Jack Haydn scowled at her with his classic father scowl. "Oh, great—you and Rosie. I'm sure a desperate killer will leave you alone because you dragged Rosie along."

Piper reached up to hug her father and kissed his cheek. "I'm fine, Daddy. Honestly."

Jack wrapped his arms around Piper and squeezed. "I can't handle anything happening to you," he whispered.

Piper squeezed back. "I know, but nothing's going to happen. Get that out of your mind. Trust in the Lord with all your heart, right?"

Jack Haydn rolled his eyes. "Don't quote scripture to me, missy." He tightened his hug and let go of Piper.

"Hey, Mr. Haydn," Rosie said.

"Roosevelt, my daughter says you'll keep her safe. How do you propose to do that?"

Rosie jumped around the room, flailing her arms and kicking. Her earrings jingled, and her palazzo pants flashed bits of color as she spun around the room.

Jack Haydn stepped back when Rosie's spinning back kick swung dangerously close to his nose. He raised his eyebrows. "Very impressive, Roosevelt. When did you learn martial arts?"

Rosie giggled. "I didn't, but no one needs to know."

Jack raked a hand through his hair and rolled his eyes. "Listen to me, both of you. Stay out of this." He pointed to Piper. "If you don't listen to me, Piper Grace, I will forcibly carry you to the house and lock you in 'til this blows over. Do you understand me?"

"Daddy, you're not going to kidnap me, and you know it." Piper patted her dad's arm. "We will stay safe. I promise. Isn't Mom waiting for you?"

Jack Haydn kissed Piper's forehead and sighed. "Nothing in the parent manual prepared me for my little girl dealing with a murder."

"Nothing at Juilliard prepared me for finding a body in my Steinway, so I guess we're even, Daddy. Go home and relax. I'm fine."

Jack nodded at the girls. "Lock the door when I leave."

"Yes, sir." Piper saluted her father and blew him a kiss.

Rosie smiled when the door closed. "That's sweet. I wish my dad watched out for me."

Piper squeezed her friend. "I'm thankful. I truly am. I wish they'd remember I'm not a baby anymore, though. Can you write down all the clues while I change?"

"I'm writing 'Lisa' all over the notebook. I still feel she's involved, Piper."

Piper hurried upstairs, her mind whirling with unanswered questions. She unwound the violet scarf and gazed at her reflection while brushing her hair. She spun around to glance out her window and shivered as she ran to pull the shade.

"Something happen up there?" Rosie called.

"Yeah. When I looked in the mirror, I imagined someone watching me. My mind's working overtime—that's all."

"If someone's up there watching you, it's a ghost. How would someone get up that high?"

"I know, Rosie. My imagination went wild, and I got the creeps for a minute."

"Writing it down," Rosie called, and her laugh floated upstairs.

Piper sighed and smiled, thankful for her childhood friend. She sat on the side of her bed and glanced around her room. The broken frog she stepped on that morning sat on the table near her closet. When she picked the frog up, the glass crumbled, and shards and a sticky substance stuck to her fingers. "That's weird."

She frowned. "I'm losing my marbles because I don't remember gluing that frog back together." She took a deep breath, swiped the remaining pieces of the broken frog into the trash, and washed her hands.

CHAPTER FOUR

Friday

P iper called the bank to verify her account balance. It was $9,738 lower than she expected. She sighed and dialed Chief Maxwell.

"Maxwell," his deep voice rumbled.

"Chief Maxwell, this is Piper Haydn. I called the bank, and there's almost $10,000 missing."

"The amount from your fundraising account?"

"Yes, sir," Piper said.

"Good work. I'll check on this. Your academy can open on Monday if you're ready. My officers finished there today, and the cleaning crew was already working."

"Thank you. Anything else?"

"No interviewing people."

Piper sighed.

"I mean it." His voice carried a warning. "Do you hear me?"

"Loud and clear, but I want to know who did this and why. I want my life back," she whispered.

"I understand, Miss Haydn, but the investigation is my job, not yours. I'm serious."

"Oh, do you have any information on how Daniel died?"

"Nothing I can share at the moment," he said.

Piper mustered her courage. "Am I a suspect, Chief Maxwell?" Piper shuffled and waited. "Sir?"

"I am not at liberty to discuss the manner of death, suspects, or information."

A shiver slithered up Piper's spine. "You mean I *am?*"

Chief Maxwell blew out a breath. "Listen, Miss Haydn, let me do my job. Please?"

"Yes, sir." Piper hung up the phone and plopped onto a stool at the kitchen counter. She wrapped her fingers around a mug full of the tea Maisy had talked her into last night. The lemon balm eased her nerves, but tea was no match for frayed emotions.

What will I do, God? This mess is too big.

She sipped tea and tried to plan for her day, but her mind churned and snarled with pieces of the mystery. She leaned her head onto her hands and fell asleep.

Piper startled and glanced at the clock. She stared out the window over the sink, trying to clear her brain, but confusion clogged her mind, and her body ached. She grabbed her phone and poured out the cold tea.

The cut on her foot ached as she hobbled through the hall to her favorite room. Light poured through the windows and shone on the music book resting on the piano. She slid onto the bench and played "Claire de Lune." The gentle music and flowing rhythm filled her with peace. She smiled, but the high C made an odd clinking sound again. She groaned and whispered, "Write that down and call the piano tuner."

A dwindling group of reporters camped out at the end of her driveway. She smiled. *You're wasting your time out there, folks.*

Her phone rang. "Morning, Rosie. Where are you? I've already called the bank, taken a nap, and practiced the piano."

Rosie laughed. "Wow. I woke up ten minutes ago. Late night."

"Why?"

"Painting and making plans for summer classes. Then my brain got running, and I couldn't stop. Where to today?"

"The academy for sure, then we can decide from there. Chief Maxwell said we could resume classes on Monday. He also said to stay out of the investigation."

"You're not listening to him, are you?"

"No. I want to know who did this and why."

"That's my girl," Rosie said. "Want me to bring Sweetberry's chocolate?"

"Ugh. No. I ate three scones while I drank the tea Maisy sent along. But I'll take coffee from Ruby's."

"Coming right up," Rosie said, and Piper settled onto the couch to return messages and emails. She emailed the parents, announcing that lessons resumed on Monday and then hurried to dress before Rosie arrived with coffee.

Piper searched her closet for an outfit Rosie would find acceptable, but her wardrobe leaned to the plain side. After grabbing a pink broomstick skirt and floral top with a coordinating scarf, she put the skirt on, twisted the scarf around her neck, tucked in the ends, and fluffed her hair.

"I might not be zany, Rosie Hale, but at least I'm not frumpy."

As Piper waited for Rosie, her mind wandered. Her jumbled brain left her unsettled. She wasn't a wishy-washy person, but she didn't recognize herself these days. Exhaustion and confusion upset her in more ways than one. She picked at the upholstery on the old couch and sighed. "I want my life back."

As she glanced at the reporters outside, wishing they would investigate the murder rather than waste time in her driveway—an urge to open her door and spill her guts fought against her better judgment.

"I need to dust," she said. Dust particles floated in the sunlight and settled on her piano. She frowned and jumped up. A green porcelain frog perched on a windowsill across the room. Piper turned the piece over and examined the frog, but nothing stood out. "Where are these coming from? It's like the plagues of Egypt!"

Rosie knocked on the window and held up the coffee cups. "Let me in!" she hollered.

Piper opened the door and grabbed a coffee. "Come here. I need to show you something."

Rosie followed Piper into the sitting room. "What?"

Piper held up the frog and pointed. "I found this on the windowsill."

Rosie grabbed the frog and turned it in her hands. She glanced at Piper. "Are you okay? I mean *really* okay?"

Piper grabbed the frog. "Are you saying I'm crazy? Do you believe I planted these here?"

Rosie frowned. "No, but it's all so odd. Did you tell hunky Mr. Police Chief?"

Piper rested her hands on her hips and glared. "I said quit calling him that, and no. What can I say? 'Oh, by the way, I've found some glass frogs.' He'd lock me up for being ridiculous."

"I don't know what to tell you. What did the bank say?"

"The money's gone."

"I told you it's Lisa. I never liked her in the first place." Rosie said.

"You never said that before, Rosie. You're upset."

"Yes, I'm upset. Someone is after my best friend, and I won't allow it."

Piper hugged Rosie and smiled. "Thank you, Rosie." She stepped back and examined her friend. "Where did you find this outfit?"

"Amazing, isn't it?" Rosie twirled, and the pleated skirt floated out and fell in graceful lines around her ankles. "Thrift store. Where else? I told you to check it out."

"Your blouse from there too?" Piper raised her eyebrows. "A *pirate* shirt?"

Rosie nudged Piper with her elbow. "I know you love it 'cause you're teasing me."

"It's perfect for you." Piper smiled. "What stops are we making today? My mind's shot, and I can't think."

Rosie settled onto the sofa, gathering the skirt under her legs. "What about questioning the business owners downtown?"

Piper nodded. "Good plan."

"And I have a stop too." Rosie's eyes sparkled. "You'll see. Grab your coffee, and let's go. I have the new notebook in my purse. We'll take my car, so you don't have to drive with your sore foot."

"Good idea—thank you. Whatever would I do without you, Roosevelt?"

"Have a lot less fun," Rosie said with a laugh.

Piper switched off the radio in Rosie's car and sighed. "Seriously, girl—you need to get better taste in music."

"Piper, you've worked on me since high school. My tastes won't change, so you enjoy your stuffy composers and arias, and I'll enjoy my country music."

"You get your dog back. You get your truck back." Piper teased and held up her hands to fend off Rosie's fake blows.

"Downtown?"

"Yes, and the academy."

"Any word from Lisa yet?" Rosie asked, and Piper shook her head. "With the missing money and her lack of communication, you better suspect her. What did Hunky Maxwell say?"

"Rosie," Piper shouted, and a red blush crept up her cheeks.

Rosie hooted. "Aha! You're blushing because you finally acknowledge his hunkiness. Come on— admit it."

"I'll do nothing of the sort, and I'm not blushing. I'm wearing pink. I always look flushed when I wear pink."

"Whatever you need to tell yourself, friend." Rosie parked her car at one end of Main Street. "Wooly Llama first?"

"Sure." Piper hopped out of the car with the notebook and slung her pink Chanel bag over her shoulder.

"Can you walk that far?" Rosie asked, glancing at Piper's bandaged foot.

"My foot feels much better. Now it only bothers me if I step wrong. Let's go."

A woman came out of The Wooly Llama as they reached for the door. Piper glanced up. "Mom?"

"Piper." Sarah Haydn hugged her. "You holding up? Your father's not happy you didn't sleep at home." She leaned in and kissed Piper's cheek.

"I'm fine, Mom. Tired and confused."

"Oh, baby—I'm sorry. Have you solved the mystery? Your father said that Chief Maxwell told you to quit poking around." Sarah glanced around Main Street. "Is that what you're doing? You don't knit." She raised her eyebrows. "Piper Grace?"

Rosie grabbed Piper's arm. "I need some yarn, Mrs. Haydn." She winked at Piper.

"I don't care if you *are* investigating. Someone needs to fix this, but your father will be inconsolable if you get hurt, so watch yourself."

Piper smiled and squeezed her mom. "I know. Thanks, Mom."

Sarah kissed Piper's forehead and smiled. "Toodles, girls."

Piper and Rosie stepped into an explosion of color. Yarn bins lined the walls, sorted by color, and Piper grabbed a skein of bright red yarn, rubbing the soft fiber.

"That's a lovely yarn, Piper. I didn't know you knit." Cassidy Barnes stepped from behind the counter.

"Not me. Mom knits, as you know." Piper smiled at the owner.

"She's my best customer. No kidding." Cassidy smiled.

"We want to know if you've seen or heard anything," Rosie said. She gripped a small basket loaded with yarn.

Cassidy frowned. "I'm so sorry, Piper. I can't imagine."

Tears stung the back of Piper's eyes at Cassidy's kindness. She wiped them away. "I don't know why I'm crying."

"Oh, girl, I'd be a blubbering mess if I had to carry your stress." She patted Piper on the arm. "To answer your question, no. I haven't noticed suspicious tourists or seen anything odd."

"Have you felt someone watching you?" Rosie asked.

Cassidy pursed her lips. "Now that you mention it, maybe. The other night I locked up after everyone left, and the air seemed off. You know when you're in the middle of a scary movie and the air vibrates and you want to scream, 'Run!'?"

Rosie nodded. "Yes, and then I pray for them and have to remind myself it's just a movie."

Cassidy laughed. "Something like that, yes. When I turned around, I didn't see anything. No cats in the alley. No strange cars on the street." She frowned. "Overactive imagination, which is easy to do with all these goings-on around here. I never imagined dealing with a murder in this beautiful town. Who'd do something so awful?"

"That's what we want to find out," Rosie said.

"Well, you two—be careful." Cassidy grabbed a skein of yarn and untwisted it. She glanced out the window.

Piper followed her gaze. "Anything else?" she asked.

"No," Cassidy said. "But tell Lisa her yarn order came in. I called several times and left messages, but she never returned my call."

Rosie raised her eyebrows and mouthed, "I told you."

Piper opened her purse. "I'll pay for Lisa's yarn, Cassidy. It gives me an excuse to swing by her house."

"Oh," Cassidy said. "Mrs. Schmidt came in yesterday and told everyone in the store that you're involved. She says you did it for free publicity for your music academy."

"For crying out loud!" Rosie yelled. "Piper, you need to kick her child out and tell her off!"

Piper smiled. "Not a good way to run a business." She pinched the bridge of her nose and rubbed her forehead. "What did everyone say?"

"No one took her bait, and Maisy was in here picking up her yarn order. She told Mrs. Schmidt off in no uncertain terms," Cassidy said.

"Good, and I'm next." Rosie huffed.

"What a mess!" Piper sighed.

Cassidy patted Piper's arm. "You're going survive this chaos with flying colors. All the prayer chains in town have you at the top of their lists. We love you, hon. Let's get this yarn rung up before my knitting class. You should join us, Piper."

Piper smiled. "Maybe when I solve this murder and finish my house renovations."

Cassidy laughed. "You'll be old and gray by the time you get that poor house in order."

"Hey," Piper said. "Don't make fun of my painted lady. All she needs is a little love."

"And a new roof, and a . . ." Rosie trailed off when Piper slugged her arm.

"What's your opinion on the 'someone's watching me' feeling everyone describes?" Rosie asked when they stepped out of the store.

"I don't know. Is it nerves, or is someone out here terrorizing the town? How much did you spend in there?" Piper said.

Rosie held up the bag. "Fifty bucks."

"Fifty dollars on yarn?"

"For my business, and if I remember correctly, you spent $80,000 on one tool for your business." Rosie rolled her eyes.

"Touché." Piper held up the bag of Lisa's yarn. "And yet another 'Lisa is missing' event."

"I don't like it at all." Rosie frowned.

"I don't either, but I don't know what to do."

"You told the hunky police chief, right?"

"Rosie—stop calling him that," Piper said.

"Right. So you told the gorgeous police chief, right?" Rosie giggled.

Piper rolled her eyes. "Oh, my word, Roosevelt Hale. And yes, I told him."

"Sweetberry's next. Sure you don't need chocolate?"

"*Need* and *want* are two different things, and I need to fit into my clothes, so no chocolate."

"You know you wanna." Rosie grinned. "I don't eat chocolate *any* day, but I know all about *you* and your chocolate addiction. Plus, whenever you outgrow your wardrobe, I can talk you into shopping at the thrift store with me." She twirled, and the skirt floated around her ankles.

Piper grabbed the door handle of Sweetberry's. The air heavy with chocolate and sugar stopped Piper in her tracks, and she took a deep breath. "Mmm. You're incorrigible, by the way, Rosie."

"At your service, ma'am." Rosie laughed and followed Piper into the bakery.

The chatter inside Sweetberry's Bakery stopped when Piper entered. Some people stared, others turned away, and a few grabbed their bags and left. Piper glanced around the room, searching for a friendly face.

"Piper!" Dominque Landry called. "I'm glad you're here!" The woman wiped her hands on the apron and hurried from behind the counter. "Have you heard from Lisa? She ordered a cake, and I called to ask her when she planned to pay for her order, but she never returned my call."

Piper frowned. "No, I haven't heard from Lisa, but I'll pass the message along when I do."

Dominique wrapped her brown arms around Piper. "How are you doin', sugar?" She stepped back and stared at Piper. "I mean, are you truly all right? I'm worried for you."

"Thank you, Mrs. Landry. I'm as well as you'd expect in this situation."

Dominique frowned. "Never thought I'd hear such awful happenings in Cranberry Harbor. Shameful."

"Have you seen or heard anything odd?" Rosie asked.

Dominique rested her hands on her hips and raised her eyebrows. "I haven't, but I'm ready to interview people myself. What are the police doing? Shouldn't take this long."

"You'll call Piper if you remember anything?" Rosie asked.

"Of course, sugar. You ladies want a treat to go?"

Piper rested her hand on her stomach. "Not me. I've been drowning my sorrows in carbs, and I need a break."

Dominique smiled. "Well, don't stay away too long. Triple chocolate brownies every day next week. I'm working through recipes deciding what to offer next holiday season."

Piper groaned. "Why'd you have to say 'triple chocolate,' Dominique? You know I can't resist."

Dominique smiled. "Gotta pay the bills somehow, darlin'."

Piper followed Rosie out the door. "Oh, hello, Mrs. Watson. I'm sending an email to let everyone know we can resume classes next Monday. I . . ." Piper frowned when the woman shoved past her into the bakery. The door shut, and the little bell over the door jingled.

"Did she . . .?"

"Yes." Rosie nodded.

"Good grief. What's going on? Did you see how everyone looked at me in Sweetberry's?" Piper asked.

"I didn't notice anything too different, but the vibe wasn't friendly. Dominique seemed the same sweetheart as ever," Rosie said.

"Mrs. Landry is a dear. She and Robby would support me even if I were guilty."

Rosie laughed. "Don't let the small-minded people bother you. Where to next?"

"How about Lillie's? After that, can you drop me off at the academy? I'll send the emails and make sure we're ready to roll next week."

"You'll stay at the academy alone?" Rosie asked, her brows raised.

"You said you needed to stop somewhere?"

Rosie waved her hand. "I'll stop another time. I'm not leaving you alone at the academy. Your dad would chew me out anyway."

"Thanks," Piper whispered.

"Hey, Piper? You all right?"

Piper nodded and wiped her eyes. "I'm so thankful for you." She grabbed Rosie and hugged her. "I can't imagine my life now if I hadn't sat by you on the playground that day."

Rose patted her back. "I'm glad you did."

Piper sighed. "I'm good now."

"What other businesses should we check out on Main Street? I know we don't have time today, but what about tomorrow? Someone must know something," Rosie said.

Piper glanced around the street. "Ruby's and the antique shop. I don't know where else to stop. We can't talk to everyone anyway."

A police car rolled down the street and stopped near Lillie's. Chief Maxwell stepped out.

"Oh, no," Piper whispered.

"Ladies," he said, his face stern. "Investigating?" he raised his eyebrows.

Rosie held up her bag of yarn. "Shopping."

Piper swallowed and held up Lisa's bag. "Yarn." She cleared her throat, ashamed of her lie.

Chief Maxwell nodded.

"Hey, have you investigated the warehouse at Notes? And what's Daniel's manner of death? Why is this taking so long?" Rosie fired questions at the man.

Piper grimaced and set her hand on Rosie's arm. "Rosie," she said.

Rosie pulled away from Piper's grasp. "I want to know, Piper, and I'm a citizen of Cranberry Harbor. I'm allowed to ask."

Chief Maxwell cleared his throat. "Yes, ma'am, you're allowed to ask, but I'm not at liberty to divulge that information. How do you know anything about Notes's warehouse? You said you are out shopping." He stared at Rosie.

"We're shopping today, and our friend works at Notes. We stopped to see his children's class the other day." Rosie raised her chin and stared at Chief Maxwell. "So why is your investigation taking so long?"

Chief Maxwell nodded. "I understand it feels long, but life isn't a *CSI* episode, Miss Hale."

"Is there any information *I'm* entitled to?" Piper asked.

He stared at her and shook his head. Piper turned away, confused by the fluttering butterflies in her stomach when she looked into his deep brown eyes.

Rosie grabbed her arm. "Excuse us, sir. We need to check out the dresses at Lillie's. You understand?"

He nodded and turned back to the police cruiser. "I meant it, ladies. No investigating." He slid behind the wheel and pulled away from the curb.

Rosie saluted him and giggled. "I totally saw you blush when he looked at you."

"Stop it," Piper whined. "We don't know anything about him."

"Other than he's hunky and has amazing brown eyes." Rosie laughed.

"I'll disown you, Roosevelt." Piper grabbed the door of Lillie's and shot Rosie a warning glance. "Behave."

"Piper, Rosie—how good to see you." Lillie Sullivan hurried toward them and gathered both into a bear hug. "How are you? It's so awful. I can't believe it. I'm sorry I didn't call you, but I didn't want to bother you."

"Don't worry, Lillie. I understand," Piper said.

"I saw you and that gorgeous officer talking out there. Isn't he delicious?" Lillie asked and waggled her eyebrows.

Piper rolled her eyes.

"Oh, he's a hunk. Piper blushes when he's near," Rosie said.

"Rosie!" Piper hollered.

Lillie and Rosie laughed, and Piper turned to examine the clothing racks. She had told the chief she was shopping, so purchasing something here might relieve her conscience.

"What do you know about him?" Rosie asked.

"The police station is around the corner, so I see him drive down Main Street pretty often. But other than that, all I know is that he's new and gorgeous," Lillie said.

"Doesn't Quinn Harper work at the police station? You're her friend. Call and ask her for the scoop," Rosie said. "Come on, girl—get with it."

"I'll call her this week and fill you in," Lillie said with a laugh.

"You hear that, Piper? News forthcoming!" Rosie hollered across the store.

"I can't hear either one of you!" Piper said and searched the racks.

Rosie pulled out the notebook. "Have you noticed anything odd? Have any information for us? Seen any weird characters?"

"Ooh, are you two Nancy Drews investigating?" Lillie asked.

"Shhh." Rosie held her finger on her lips. "Mr. Hunky police chief forbid us from investigating, but we can't help it."

"Of course not—it's Piper's life," Lillie said. "I haven't seen or heard much other than everyone is uneasy and worried. It's hard to believe a murderer is out there walking among us, and we don't know who." Lillie crossed her arms and shivered.

"It's not one of us." Piper turned from the rack. "I don't know anyone savage enough to take a life and leave it in my piano. Someone who doesn't live in our beautiful town did this. No one who loves Cranberry Harbor would ruin our peace." She turned to the rack, her hands shaking.

Lillie nodded. "I agree. I don't know anyone capable of committing a crime so awful. It has to be a tourist. I've not noticed anyone out of place, though."

"Do you think someone passing through town murdered him? We *are* close to the interstate," Rosie said.

"Exactly. Piper, that color is amazing for you. We got a scarf order yesterday. If you want to check them out, I'll grab the box. I haven't priced anything yet."

"Sure," Piper said, dropping the blouse onto the counter.

Rosie grabbed the price tag. "Forty dollars for a T-shirt? You seriously need to shop at the Cranberry Closet with me."

"Shh," Piper hushed her friend as Lillie came out of the back room with a box. Piper grabbed a scarf with fireworks and "USA" in elegant print. "Add this one and the shirt, and tell me my total."

Lillie rang up Piper's order and folded the items in peach tissue paper. She tied a ribbon around the packages and slid them into a floral bag. "Be careful, you two. Promise me."

Piper and Rosie nodded. "I promise, Lillie. Don't worry."

Rosie grabbed the notebook and hurried behind Piper. "And call me with whatever you discover about Chief Hunky!" she called over her shoulder. Rosie bumped into Piper. "Why are you just standing there?"

Piper pointed at a bright green frog on the hood of Rosie's car.

Rosie turned and ran back inside Lillie's. "Lillie, show me your security tape."

Lillie's eyes widened. "I don't have one."

"What? All this merchandise sitting here, and you don't have security cameras?" Rosie shrieked.

"It's Cranberry Harbor. No one has security tapes. Why?" Lillie said.

Rosie blew out her breath. "I'll tell you later. Sorry I yelled." Rosie ran out the door to find Piper staring at the frog. "Should we call the police?" Rosie said.

"No. What would I say? 'I keep finding frogs'? They'll laugh at me." Piper marched to Rosie's car and grabbed the frog. "We'll figure this out on our own, Rosie." She turned and glanced up Main Street before plopping into Rosie's passenger seat.

Rosie parked in the empty parking lot of Haydn Music Academy. Piper smiled at her and hopped out of the car. "I'll email staff and parents and double-check a few details. I don't need long."

"Perfect," Rosie said. "I'll double-check that all of the rooms are in order and putter around in my classroom."

Piper flipped on all the lights in the entryway and locked the door. She stood and glanced around. "Spending time in the academy used to bring me joy and contentment, but now I'm shaking like a leaf in here."

Rosie hugged her. "Piper, don't be so hard on yourself. This whole mess is confusing and traumatic, and you're handling this like any normal person. I'd hide in my house if I were you."

Piper smiled. "Thanks for the pep talk. Find me in the office later?"

Rosie nodded and scurried down the hall, singing at the top of her lungs.

"Roosevelt!" Piper called. "You're not desecrating my halls with country music, are you?"

Rosie's laugh echoed down the hall. "Who, me? Never!"

Piper smiled and hurried to her office, turning on every light she passed. She plopped into her chair and turned on the computer, composing the emails in her mind. Her full inbox occupied her for an hour. She calmed anxious parents by sending polite emails to assure them that the academy would return to normal very soon.

After sending an email to all parents and staff, Piper rested her head in her hands. "God, can you please help the police solve this soon? Give me strength and help me trust that you're in control."

---Almost done, Rosie. Meet me at the door?

--Ok, give me 5.

Piper hurried to the front door flipping lights off as she passed. She held her breath as dread tumbled in her belly.

How will I ever feel comfortable in my academy again?

Piper's heart pounded, and she glanced behind her, feeling eyes watching her. Her breath came in short gasps, and she ran. Tears pressed the back of her eyes, but Piper refused to let them fall. "I don't know who you are or why you did this, but you won't win," she whispered through gritted teeth.

When she reached the lobby, Rosie turned. "Whoa—what's wrong?"

Piper stopped and put her hands on her knees, gulping air. "I don't know how I'll ever feel safe here, Rosie. My office was fine, but when I walked down the hall turning off lights, I expected someone to jump out or grab me."

Rosie glanced around the lobby. "I pulled the shades in my classroom because I was sure someone was watching me."

Piper sighed, and a tear rolled down her cheek. "What are we going to do, Rosie?"

Rosie lifted her chin and said, "You're going to open for classes on Monday and take back your space. You'll reclaim your life and your academy, and we'll move past this horrible chapter."

"Thanks, Rosie." Piper wiped her eyes. "Let me peek at the auditorium. The cleaners did a good job—everything's in order."

Piper took a deep breath and tugged the heavy wooden door open. She flipped on the lights and glanced around the area. Instead of a shiny new Steinway, her old grand piano sat on the stage. Piper walked down the center aisle and relaxed her shoulders. Tension rolled off her back. "I'm playing the piano for a few minutes, Rosie. You're right. I have to take my life back."

Piper sat at the bench and rested her fingers on the keyboard before playing warm-up scales. She poured her anger and sadness on the piano, allowing the smooth keys to restore her peace. She played "Amazing Grace" and "To God Be the Glory," then moved into Debussy's "Reverie." She closed her eyes and allowed her mind to concentrate on the music while the tension in her belly unwound. Piper took a deep breath and opened her eyes.

"Bravo, bravo! Encore!" Rosie sat in the front row clapping.

Piper grinned. "That wasn't a performance--that was sanity-saving." She pulled the cover over the keys and reached to close the lid but frowned at a flash of green peeking from behind the stage curtains.

"What?" Rosie called and followed Piper to the corner.

Piper grabbed a porcelain frog and scowled. "What *is* this? What's going on?"

"I told you that Debussy wouldn't compose without his frog, right?"

Piper nodded. "But that doesn't explain why all these frogs show up. I'm not Debussy, and I'm not composing. It's an odd coincidence but doesn't explain frogs showing up everywhere."

"Don't touch the next one and call Officer Hunky. It's past time for you to tell him," Rosie said.

Piper shot her a warning glance. "Rosie, don't call him that."

"All right, all right, but you need to tell him."

"I don't see what he'd do, and I have a feeling he'd write me off as a loony bird." Piper stuffed the frog into her purse. "Is someone sending me a message?"

"What kind of message is leaving porcelain frogs around?" Rosie asked.

"I don't know." Piper sighed. "Where did you need to stop earlier?"

Rosie's eyes sparkled. "Nowhere. I'm good."

"What are you up to?" Piper narrowed her eyes at her best friend.

"It's like you don't trust me, Piper," Rosie said and pouted.

"No, it's like I *know* you, Roosevelt Hale." Piper laughed and flipped off the lights. "I need to get home and sort this information. We can see if a comment or clue clicks into place. Do you want to come over, or do you need to get home?"

"I'll hang out with you for a bit, but I do need coffee," Rosie said.

Piper smiled. "Me too—and chocolate."

"You said you gave up chocolate." Rosie frowned.

"I did this morning, but . . ."

Rosie laughed and followed Piper to the car.

Piper plopped onto the couch with her large latte from Ruby's. Rosie perched on an overstuffed chair across the room, sipping black coffee.

"Don't you sit anywhere else in this massive house?" Rosie asked.

Piper smiled. "The turret is my favorite, plus look at all that sun."

Trefor knocked on the window, and Rosie jumped. "Oh, goodness! He scared me!"

"He got me the other day too, but I was asleep." Piper laughed and opened the door for Trefor.

He held up a large coffee. "Oh, you have coffee already?" He frowned.

Piper grabbed a cup. "I *always* need coffee. Thanks, Trefor. How was your day?"

He smiled and tugged at his pant leg. "Today is a good day because I have my Elvis socks on."

Rosie raised an eyebrow. "Which totally matches your Hawaiian shirt." She rolled her eyes.

Trefor frowned. "What are you trying to say, Rosie?"

Piper pointed to the other end of the couch, hoping to diffuse an argument. "Sit, Trefor. Your socks are great." She shot a warning glance to Rosie, who zipped her lips with exaggerated movements.

Trefor sat and adjusted his slouchy hat. "Lots of upset people in town. People wonder why the police aren't sharing more, why Haydn money buys privacy."

Piper frowned. "What are you *saying*, Trefor?" Her voice rose an octave.

He glanced up. "Just repeating what I heard." He grabbed a bottle out of his pocket and slathered hand sanitizer up his arms and over his hands, wincing when the alcohol hit his paper cut. "Lots of scared people in Cranberry Harbor."

"My father's money has nothing to do with police silence. They don't even share information with me, and Daniel was in *my* Steinway, for crying out loud!" She paced. "I'm sick to death of people acting like my family is the enemy because we have money.

My father worked hard for his money." She pointed at Trefor and said, "And for the record, this town wouldn't be a thriving tourist attraction without my father's money."

Trefor held up his hands. "I'm not saying those things, but some people believe his money shields you."

"Who's 'some people,' Trefor? Spit out names," Rosie said.

"Whoa, ladies! I didn't come here for you to grill me!" He stood up, his eyes flashing and his cheeks red.

Rosie pointed to the door. "Then get out."

Trefor marched to the door, his Birkenstocks smacking on the wood floor. "Piper, I'll stop another time when you don't have company." He stared at Rosie and slammed Piper's front door.

"Good riddance." Rosie peeked out the window. "He has a temper, doesn't he?"

"You two pick at each other like children," Piper said. "He means well."

"Insulting my best friend's family doesn't fly with me." Rosie scowled.

"And I love you for that. You're adorable." Piper blew a kiss to Rosie and sank back into the cushions.

Rosie grabbed her keys. "Call me if you need me later. I need to run and set up my art class. We're painting a summer tree with the four-year-olds."

"Good luck," Piper said and chuckled. "I wouldn't touch that project with a ten-foot pole."

Rosie laughed. "Well, I wouldn't attempt teaching a four-year-old how to play the piano, so we're even."

Piper smiled, and Rosie's laughter echoed back to Piper as she left. Time to put the puzzle together.

Piper sank on the couch and rested her head. She closed her eyes, enjoying the quiet of a reporter-free neighborhood. When she returned home this afternoon, the street and end of her driveway were empty. Piper sighed, thankful for the reprieve.

Piper grabbed the notebook and read Rosie's scribbled notes. "This is nonsense," she whispered. She replayed the conversations with business owners and friends but didn't recognize a common thread. The strange feelings people shared didn't offer a solid clue, and nothing blended into a cohesive hypothesis.

She tossed the notebook aside. "Feelings won't solve murders." She remembered Chief Maxwell's warning. "If my sanity didn't depend on solving Daniel's murder, I *would* stay out of it, Chief."

The sunset shone through her old bubbled windows. Piper smiled and whispered, "From the rising of the sun unto the going down of the same, the Lord's name is to be praised."

What do I praise you for in this terrible mess, God?

She sat still enjoying the sunset until peace flooded her heart. "God. I'll praise you for peace and that beautiful sunset. Thank you."

She checked her phone for a return call or text from Lisa. Nothing. Piper jumped up and grabbed her keys. "That's it, Lisa. Where are you?"

Nighttime in Cranberry Harbor was Piper's favorite. Lights hung around patios and fences, and lit store windows decorated Main Street. The town oozed charm day and night, but Piper loved the cheerful sight of all the lights. She always enjoyed a drive through town after dark, but she gripped the steering wheel tonight and scanned side streets and alleys. She imagined a villain behind every shadow and a murderer at every corner.

Piper's mind raced, and her stomach churned. "Not your brightest idea, Piper." She drove past the Haydn orchards, resisting the urge to park in the farthest orchard and scream her frustrations to the sky. "Might help," she whispered.

She parked in Lisa's driveway and glanced at her surroundings. Lisa's home sat on the edge of town bordering the countryside, where street lights seemed dim and farther apart. Piper frowned, and her heart pounded. She took several deep breaths and jumped out of the car.

A shiver ran up Piper's spine at the dark house and dim streetlights. She hugged herself and rubbed her cold arms. Turning in a slow circle, she checked Lisa's yard and driveway. The scent of new-mown grass caught Piper's attention, and she stepped onto the lawn. Clippings rested on top of the grass. *Who mowed if she's not here?* Piper straightened and gripped her keys at a rustling behind the house. *What are you doing? You can't protect yourself.*

She tiptoed between the garage and house and peeked around the corner. Lisa stood at the pen feeding the goats, and Piper gasped.

Lisa whirled around, dropping the bucket of feed, her eyes wide. She reached down to grab the bucket and ran.

Piper ran behind her and yelled, "Lisa. Lisa. Stop. Tell me what's happening!"

Lisa turned to Piper. "You shouldn't be here, Piper! Go away!" She jumped into a car parked behind the house and peeled out of the driveway.

Piper stood in the dark yard and glanced around. "Who's out there? What's going on?" she yelled.

Goats bleated in their pen, and a chicken squawked—their voices loud in the quiet evening air. Piper walked back to her car, confusion fogging her mind, and slid behind the wheel. She rested her hand on her chest to calm her heartbeat and reached into her purse for her keys. She snatched her hand back and stared.

A green porcelain frog perched on top of her wallet. She glanced around the yard. Was someone standing in the shadows near the porch? Her hands shook as she tried to start the car, and she held back a sob.

"Come on, Piper. Overactive imagination—that's all." She backed out of Lisa's driveway and pointed the car toward home, chattering to herself to settle her nerves.

"Get home. That's all you need, Piper. Go home and go to bed." Her teeth chattered, and she switched the heat to high. Laughter bubbled up, and she bit it back. "Stop, Piper. You're going crazy."

Red and blue lights shone in her mirror.

Piper rolled down her window as the man reached her door.

"Miss Haydn?"

Piper glanced up into Chief Maxwell's face and groaned. "Sir."

"Why are you in such a hurry this evening?" He leaned down and peered into her window. "Miss Haydn? What's going on?" He pointed his flashlight in the car and craned his neck toward the back seat. "Why are you shaking?"

Piper bit her lip.

"Miss Haydn, please answer my question. What are you doing out here this evening?"

"I stopped to check on Lisa," Piper whispered.

His eyebrows rose. "What do you mean you checked on Lisa?"

"She hasn't answered any texts or calls, and I'm worried, so I hopped in the car and drove out to her home."

Chief Maxwell clenched his fist. "Unbelievable. I told you to step back and stay out of my investigation. Is that so difficult to understand?"

"No, sir."

"What did you see at Lisa's?" he asked.

"The house was dark, but I heard her goats and walked back to the pen. Lisa was there."

"What? Why didn't you call me?" Chief Maxwell stepped away from the car and spoke into his radio. "What did she say?"

"Lisa said I shouldn't be there and ran to her car and peeled off. Then I worried that I saw someone in the shadows and got spooked, so I jumped into my car and sped into town, and you pulled me over."

Chief Maxwell raised his eyebrows. "Did you see which direction she drove?"

"No." Piper frowned. "I'm sorry."

He stared until she flinched. "Well, you *should* be sorry, Miss Haydn. You're free to go." He turned on his heel and marched back to his cruiser.

Piper blew out a shaky breath and rested her head on the wheel.

"Miss Haydn, is there a problem?" Chief Maxwell's cruiser stopped next to her car.

"No, sir."

"Then go home. Now." The cruiser drove off, and Piper pulled away from the curb, her hands shaking and her head pounding.

"I've stepped in it now," she whispered.

Piper drove home, watching her speedometer. "I do not need another meeting with Chief Maxwell." She rolled her eyes and mimicked, "'Unbelievable—didn't I tell you to stay out of this?'" His brisk demands annoyed Piper. "Just so you know, I *can't* stay out of this. I have too much at stake."

She pulled into her driveway and glanced around. "I forgot to leave the lights on," she said and sighed. Goosebumps rose on her arms, and she glanced around the yard again. "Quit it, Piper. Walk inside your house and climb into bed." She grabbed her purse and pointed her house key between her fingers.

If anyone jumps me, I'll key them.

She took a deep breath and ran for her door, slamming the bolt locked. She leaned on the door and closed her eyes for a moment. Her phone buzzed.

--Meeting of The Core 8 a.m. Don't be late. Dad

She groaned. "Eight, Dad? Ugh. Why do I come from a family of early birds?" She unwound her scarf and kicked her shoes under the counter. "Time for bed before I turn into a pumpkin."

Piper curled up in bed and checked her email before turning out the light. Piper answered several disgruntled parents and questions from staff and dropped her phone onto the side table. Her eyelids heavy, she drifted into a fitful sleep, dreaming of speeding cars, chiding police officers, and villains lurking in shadows.

CHAPTER FIVE

Saturday

P iper gave up on sleep at five o'clock and padded downstairs for coffee. "I'd kill for one of Ruby's super-size lattes right now," she said, switching on the coffee pot. "Take that back. No killing around here. You hear that, hunky officer?" Heat rose in Piper's cheeks, and she groaned. "Rosie, you're rubbing off on me," she whispered to the empty kitchen.

Piper tapped on her Debussy playlist, and music filled the sitting room. She plopped onto her favorite corner of the couch with the mug of steaming coffee. "Well, I enjoyed the sunset last night. Might as well enjoy the sunrise this morning." She sipped hot coffee and let her mind wander until the phone buzzed.

--Trefor here. Need anything? A colossal coffee from Ruby's?

--Perfect. You read my mind, but I have to leave by 7:30.

--Be there in a jiffy.

Piper smiled. She loved Ruby's heavy-duty extra-large coffee. A text from Rosie interrupted her dreams of coffee and energy.

--Sleep, ok?

--No, and I have a meeting with The Core in a bit.
--Should I swing by?

--Yes. Thanks, Rosie.

--Ok.

Piper dressed, choosing a pencil skirt and a ruffled white blouse. She grabbed the orange Hermes scarf her dad had given her for Christmas last year. She tied the scarf in an elegant Edot knot, arranged the fabric around her neck, and fluffed the ends.

"Yes, shameless pandering so Dad knows I'm not ignoring everything he tells me." Piper pulled a brush through her hair and smiled at her reflection. "Perfect."

Trefor and Rosie waited on the porch, peering into the window. "Sorry. I was upstairs. When did you get here?"

"Right now," Rosie said.

Trefor held out the colossal latte, and Piper grabbed the cup. She gulped the hot liquid. "Mmm . . . I feel this in my soul."

"Long night?" he asked.

"Worse than long, but forget all that. Come sit." She curled up in her favorite spot, and Rosie grabbed the chair. Trefor perched on the piano bench, stretching his long legs.

"Show me the socks," Rosie demanded.

Trefor hiked his pant leg a few inches. "Albert Einstein today."

Rosie laughed. "At least your hair doesn't match his. Speaking of *match*, that shirt doesn't match your socks."

Trefor glared at Rosie.

Piper cleared her throat. "It's Saturday—no need for matching."

"You look good with some color. Where did you get that scarf?" Rosie asked and jumped up to rub her fingers on the edge.

Piper waved her hand to keep Rosie away. "It's Hermes—don't touch it. Dad brought it home for me from Paris."

Rosie narrowed her eyes. "New or used?"

"At an antique store. Why?" Piper frowned.

"So—you *can* wear used stuff after all, huh?" Rosie teased.

"Come on, Rosie. There's a world of difference between a Hermes from Paris and some old woman's donations to the Cranberry Closet."

Rosie tossed her curls. "I find the best stuff there; besides, Cranberry Closet benefits the food pantry. Saw a shirt there the other day for you, Trefor—1990s geometric print button-up shirt in rainbow colors."

Trefor smiled. "Oh. That's definitely my kind of shirt. I'll stop and check if it's still there."

"Well, anyway, Miss "I Can't Shop Used," orange is a good color on you," Rosie said.

"I gotta run and get to The Core by eight." Piper grabbed her purse.

Rosie curled her lip. "Yikes. A Saturday morning Core meeting isn't good news. Did the police give Lenny any information?"

"Not yet." Piper glanced at her watch. "Can you two check in later? Maybe we can sit down and sort all these bits of information again."

Trefor nodded, and Rosie saluted Piper. "Oh, Lisa texted and asked what time the academy opens Monday."

Piper frowned. "She texted? What did you say?"

"Nothing. I'll leave that up to you," Rosie said.

"What's going on with Lisa?" Trefor asked.

"Too big of a story for now. If I'm late, Dad will have my head." Piper shooed her guests to the door and raced to her car.

Piper jogged through the house, taking the back way as she did when she was young. She slipped into her seat at the table as her father stepped into the room. He glanced up from a stack of papers and raised his eyebrows. "Nice scarf, Piper Grace. Glad you're on time this morning."

His secretary followed with coffee and set the mug at his spot. "Piper?" she asked.

"I'm good. I already drank a latte from Ruby's. Thank you."

Braden and Emily strolled in hand in hand, laughing. Piper glanced at Emily's rounding belly. "Emily?" she pointed at her sister-in-law's stomach.

Emily grinned. "I haven't seen you lately—sorry. I asked your parents to keep our secret."

Piper squealed and ran around the table, grabbing Emily in a bear hug. "Niece or nephew?"

"Not sure yet," Emily said with a laugh.

"Aha! I see she finally knows!" Sarah said and wrapped her arm around Braden. "I was glad you didn't ask why I bought more yarn yesterday when I saw you at Woolly Llama." Mom laughed and hugged Piper.

"I'm so excited!" Piper said and settled into her spot at the table.

Chase sauntered to his spot, his hair standing on end and his pajama pants low on his hips. He rubbed his eyes and yawned. "What's all the squealing about?"

"Your brother and Emily are having a baby, Chase. Pull your pants up." Mother kissed his cheek.

Chase grinned. "Now the kids outnumber you." He snorted and leaned back in his chair, his eyes closed.

A bubble of excitement rose in Piper's heart. "Is the baby announcement the reason for The Core meeting?" she asked.

"No," her father said. "Far from it. Fill us in, Lenny." He pointed to the attorney as he slid into his seat across the table.

Lenny shuffled a pile of papers and cleared his throat. "Well, Jack, we have news on the case." Lenny stood and passed a sheet out to each family member at the table. "Chief Maxwell called last night. First of all, there was no bomb threat at the academy. They believe in the excitement and multiple calls to 911, someone misunderstood the issue. Second, Daniel Graves's cause of death is strangulation."

Piper's stomach rolled, and she pinched the bridge of her nose while she blew out a breath. Daniel's lifeless face flashed in her mind, and tears pressed the back of her eyes.

"You okay?" Emily whispered and patted her arm.

Piper nodded, and Lenny continued. "Chief Maxwell threatened to arrest you the next time you interfere, Piper."

Piper's head jerked up into the stare of her family members. "What?" she asked.

"Piper Grace!" Her dad exploded. "I told you to stay out of this!" He blew out a breath and dropped his Urushi pen onto the table. "What were you thinking?"

Sarah Haydn patted her husband's knee. "She's thinking she wants this to end." Sarah glanced around the table. "We *all* want this to end."

Dad stared at Piper, "I never believed you'd involve yourself in a murder, Piper."

Chase choked back a laugh from the far end of the table. "Dad, someone delivered Daniel's dead body to her in her piano. She didn't go out looking for this."

Dad pointed at his youngest son and said, "Young man, you of all people need to stay out of this."

Chase sat straight, and his eyes flitted from one person to the next. "What? What are you talking about?"

Jack Haydn sighed and pointed at his attorney. "Lenny?"

Lenny cleared his throat and stared over his glasses. "Chief Maxwell notified me that the investigation has led them to a person of interest."

Piper glanced around the table. Everyone stared at Lenny.

"Well, who?" she asked, her stomach-churning.

"Chase Haydn," he said.

Questions exploded around the table, and Piper stared at her baby brother.

Oh, Chase—what have you done?

Piper glanced around the table at her family's pale faces. Chase sat at the end, holding up his hands. "Now wait a minute. I didn't do anything to Daniel." His hands shook when he reached for a glass of water.

"Oh, Chase—what did you do?" Piper whispered.

"I didn't do *anything.* I don't know what's going on." Chase stood up and pointed at Lenny. "Fix this," he screeched.

"Sit down, son," Dad said. "Lenny?"

Lenny cleared his throat. "They didn't give me any other information. They called Chase and me to an appointment downtown in half an hour." He glanced at his watch. "We need to leave. Chase?"

Chase whispered, "I need to get dressed." He ran out of the room.

"What do they say he did?" Piper asked.

Lenny frowned. "Hard to say with Chase. I don't mean any disrespect, but you all know Chase's past decisions are questionable. Do the police suspect him because he's a known troublemaker? Is someone after your family because of the money? Are they grasping at straws? I can't say." He stood and shuffled papers into his briefcase. "We have to leave. Gather Chase for me, please."

Jack nodded and left the room. Mom sat twisting a napkin in her hand, staring out the window, and Braden whispered to Emily.

"What are we going to do?" Piper asked.

Mom stood up and asked, "Coffee, anyone?"

"Mom," Braden said. "Sit down. No one wants coffee."

"Well, *I* do," Mom said, her bright pasted-on smile indicating that she was ready to fall apart.

"I'll get you coffee, Mom. Sit," Piper said.

"No. I want coffee, and I will get it myself. It's fine." She marched from the room and slammed the door.

Braden blew out a breath and said, "She's mad."

Piper nodded. "When that perky smile comes out . . ."

"She's not 'fine,'" Braden said. He grinned at Piper. "*You* okay?"

Piper nodded. "Yes, but what a mess!"

"You asked questions around town," Emily said. "Did you figure anything out?"

Piper frowned. "No, because nothing adds up. People have an odd feeling that someone is watching them. Lisa has been missing, and the academy's fundraising account is empty." She blew out a breath. "Other than that, we've discovered nothing."

Braden frowned. "I don't know what to say, but if Chief Maxwell told you to stay out of it, you need to listen, Piper. This isn't a joke."

Emily nodded. "No one wants you to get hurt."

"Rosie's been with me most of the time," Piper said.

"Most of the time?" Braden's head shot up. "What do you mean—'most of the time'?"

Piper pasted on her fake smile. "We go everywhere together. Don't worry about us."

"It's my *job* to worry about you, Piper."

"I'm not a baby, Braden." Piper glared at her brother.

"No, Piper, you're not a baby, and no one believes you are. But this isn't a party—it's a murder—and you can find yourself in a lot of trouble or danger. Please let the police handle the investigation and stay safe," Braden said.

Emily patted her round belly. "Your niece or nephew needs Auntie Piper safe and healthy."

Piper smiled. "I know you're concerned, and of course I want to meet the baby. I don't have a death wish, but how is asking a couple of questions unsafe?"

"Please, Piper," Braden said. "There's a reason they've asked you to step back. What if they know something you don't know and they're trying to keep you alive?"

Piper sighed. "I get all that, but you didn't see Daniel's dead face staring at you." She shuddered and said, "I can't explain how awful, Braden."

Emily reached over the table and patted Piper's hand. "I'm so sorry you saw that, Piper. I can't imagine. Maybe you need to talk to someone to help you process the trauma."

Piper rubbed her eyes. "No. I'm fine. I just need my life and my academy back."

Braden smirked and asked, "Is that a Sarah Haydn 'fine' or an honest 'fine'?"

"I don't know, Braden. I want to mean an honest 'fine,' but this is horrible."

Braden glanced at his watch. "Time to pack up. Soccer game for Landon at noon. Wanna come, Auntie Piper?"

Piper pouted. "Not today, but tell me when the next game is. I'll paint my face and scream his name 'til he's embarrassed."

Emily laughed. "That little guy doesn't get embarrassed. He'd love to have you cheer for him next time."

Braden wrapped his arms around Piper and gave her a bear hug. "No more poking around—promise me."

Piper nodded and reached for Emily. "Congratulations, Mama." She patted Emily's belly and said, "Grow big and strong so Auntie Piper can spoil you, baby." She smiled, "Thank you. I love you."

"We love you too." Emily blew a kiss as they left, and Piper sank onto her chair and rested her head on the table.

"You needed coffee after all." Sarah patted Piper's back.

"I don't know, Mom. Everything is a mess."

"Yes," Sarah said and sighed. "Do you believe Chase hurt Daniel?"

"I don't know, Mom. Lenny's probably correct with his theory that they brought Chase in because of his past transgressions."

"I raised that boy the same as I raised you and Braden. I don't know what happened." She smiled, but a tear rolled down her cheek.

"Oh, Mama, don't cry." Piper wiped her mom's cheek. "You did a wonderful job with us. Chase's bad choices aren't your fault, Mom. You're not to blame."

"Thank you, Piper, but I'm his mom, and I'll always doubt myself. What did I do wrong, or how did I fail him? I hold some responsibility that he's not a straight arrow like you two. I tried to keep my disappointment from him. I love him the same as I love you, but he's so stubborn. He was from the first moment we met him." Sarah smiled. "He was two weeks past his due date and born with an attitude. He always did life his way, and he spent more time in the time-out chair than the two of you combined."

Piper smiled. "He's definitely his own guy, but I don't believe he did this, Mom. He might smoke stuff he shouldn't or get loud when he and his buddies drink—but murder?"

Her mother sighed. "Well, the smoke stuff and drinking with his buddies is part of the issue."

"I know, Mom, but he's an adult. Release the guilt because you're not to blame no matter what happens," Piper said.

Mom grabbed her napkin again and dabbed her eyes. "If he murdered Daniel, I don't know how I'll survive this, Piper. I can't stand the thought of seeing my son in prison."

Piper rubbed her mom's back and squeezed her shoulders. "I don't want to visit him in prison either, but if he murdered Daniel, he has to live with the consequences. God will sustain us no matter what happens."

Mom nodded and dabbed her eyes. "I know, Piper. I know, but I'm terrified. When I married your father, I imagined smooth sailing and a life of luxury. I didn't anticipate anything as devastating as this." She blew her nose.

"I don't know how you'd prepare for this. Or how you'd plan for it. Should I pray?" Piper asked.

Mom nodded and wiped her eyes.

"God, we don't know what to say or do, but we know You see our pain. You hear our cries, and You understand our doubts. Please, help us trust You through this trial no matter what happens. Amen."

"Amen," Sarah whispered. "Thank you, sweetheart. What are you and Roosevelt doing today?"

"Rosie was at my house this morning with Trefor. They brought coffee, and she said she wanted to look at something or pick something up. I don't remember."

"Trefor?"

"That guy from the music store," Piper said.

"The long-hair, skinny jeans guy?" Mom asked. "Are he and Rosie an item?

Piper laughed and said, "Oh, Mom—if Rosie heard you say that, she might slug you. Do you mind if I play the piano a few minutes before I leave?"

"Of course not. I'll grab my coffee and listen. I've always loved listening to you play."

Piper grabbed her purse and turned back to her mom. "Is Dad disappointed I didn't join him at the orchard?"

Sarah frowned. "Disappointed? What on earth do you mean?" She asked.

Piper sighed. "Sometimes I sense he's disappointed that I opened the academy instead of helping him at the orchard. I wonder if he thinks I deserted him to do my own thing. He expected us to join him since we were small."

"Piper Grace Haydn, stop. Your father loves that you're creating your own business using your talents and skills. He loves that orchard because his father and grandfather ran it before him. But he's not disappointed in you at all. He's so proud of you."

"Is he happier with Braden because he joined the orchard? Chase and I didn't."

"Oh, Piper—you don't know your father very well if you believe that. Trust me. He's proud of you and happy that you're doing what you love. He's a bit jealous too."

"What?" Piper said. "Why is Dad jealous of me?"

Sarah laughed. "Have you ever heard your father play the piano? He's amazed that a child of his has so much musical ability. He always wanted to play, but his father didn't allow him to take lessons. 'Not enough time for following dreams,' Grandpa said. He's always let you children do what you love, and he's tickled that you play the piano so well. Braden's dream is to follow your dad and take over the orchard. Chase's dream?" She sighed and waved her hand. "No, your dad is not disappointed that you earn money playing the piano. Definitely not."

"Thank you, Mom. I never knew," Piper said.

"How long have you carried that worry?" Her mother patted Piper's arm. "You should have asked long ago, baby." She grabbed her coffee mug and followed Piper to the piano. "Let's hear some of that musical genius that cost us a fortune."

After playing several pieces, Piper kissed her mother goodbye and drove to her favorite spot on earth—the Haydn orchards. The family orchards sprawled along the outskirt of Cranberry Harbor, and Piper was free to wander to her heart's content. She parked in the back orchard and leaned against an apple tree.

Sitting under an apple tree with a book was her favorite pastime when she was a little girl. Dad brought her to work with him in the morning, and Piper ran free all day. She visited the orchard store, helped in the bakery, and read under the trees. When her brothers came to work with Dad, they ran through the orchards playing hide and seek. The breeze in the trees and chirping birds reminded her of happier days and filled her heart with peace.

Piper sighed. "If I went back in time, I'd rewrite history and leave Daniel out of my story."

How are you involved in this, Chase?

The clues she and Rosie uncovered and Chase's status as a suspect didn't clear anything in her fuzzy brain.

And where are those stupid glass frogs coming from?

Piper leaned against the tree and fell asleep dreaming of a glass frog chasing her into a Steinway and slamming the lid closed. She screamed and banged on the lid, and no one heard her. The piano wire pressed into her back, and she gasped for air. "Help me! Help me!"

"Miss Piper. Piper, are you all right?" A hand grabbed her shoulder, and Piper screamed.

"Oh, goodness, Piper! It's me—Robby!"

Piper rubbed her eyes. "I'm sorry, Robby. Dreaming, I guess." She grabbed the weathered brown hand Robby held out.

"More like a nightmare if you ask me. What are you doing out here all alone? What made you scream?" he asked.

"Something chased me into a piano and slammed the lid." Piper sighed. "I know it sounds crazy."

"Nothing crazy about that. You're dealing with a lot right now. I think your brain wants to sort everything out and figure out this ugliness," Robby said.

Piper nodded and said, "Exactly, but I'm confused, and my tired brain wants all of this to go away."

"I bet. We're all praying for you, you know." Robby patted her back. "You should head home and stay safe. Swing by Sweetberry's and tell my wife to give you one of those brownies from the new recipe she tried this morning. Tell her Robby sent you." He smiled, his deep brown eyes full of concern.

"Thanks, Robby. I better skip the brownie." Piper patted her stomach. "I've lived on junk food and coffee with all this stress." She grimaced.

Robby laughed. "Well, ask her for a hug then. You know she gives the best hugs." He patted her back. "I'll wait while you leave, Piper. I don't want you out here alone." His gaze swept around the orchard.

"Did something happen?"

"Nothing specific," Robby said. "I'm worried about you—that's all. Head on home now and keep out of trouble. You hear?"

Piper nodded and said, "Yes, sir."

He laughed. "We all love you, Piper. I remember you and your hooligan brothers running around this orchard. If anything happened to you, I'd . . ." Robby wiped his eyes.

"Robby," Piper said and patted his arm, "I'm sorry I worried you. I'll go home right now. Does that make you happy?"

He nodded.

She slipped behind the wheel of her Mercedes and waved. Robby waved and glanced around the orchard again.

Piper shivered. A cold knot twisted in her stomach. *What's going on that spooked Robby?*

She prayed out loud. "God—will you stop this confusion and fear? We all need our nice little peaceful Cranberry Harbor back without murder and mayhem, please?"

Piper pulled out onto Berry Avenue and turned toward town. "Maybe I need one of Dominque's brownies after all." She smiled and turned up the radio. Praise music filled her car, and she tapped her finger to the beat on the steering wheel.

"Cranberry Harbor police questioned suspect Chase Haydn today. The murder of Daniel Graves rocked the small town last week. The investigation continues—"

"Ugh!" Piper screamed and switched the radio off. The cold knot twisted in her belly, and tears pressed at the back of her eyes. "God," she prayed. "How is this good? I don't see your hand, but I want to trust. Help me."

She parked in front of Sweetberry's and sighed. "I need a whole lot of Jesus and a little bit of chocolate." Piper grabbed her phone.

--You two want to come over for a bit? Want anything from Sweetberry's?

--Nothing for me. Be there in 15. R.

--Finishing class. I can stop for a few later. My regular coffee, please. Trefor.

Piper hurried into Sweetberry's. "Dominique, I saw Robby at the orchard, and he said you baked a new brownie recipe today. I need two and a large latte with soy milk for Trefor."

Dominique nodded. "Sure did try a new recipe, girl, and let me tell you—it's amazing. You said you gave up carbs?" Dominique rested her hand on her hips and raised her eyebrows.

"Come on, Dominique. You know that was my stress talking," Piper said.

Dominique laughed. "For sure. Well, let me grab those. Trefor takes two pumps of vanilla, that fine?"

Piper nodded and glanced around the bakery. "Quiet in here today?"

"Morning rush and lunch crowd cleared out about five minutes ago. Here you are, sugar. I added an extra brownie on the house."

"You're the sweetest," Piper said.

"That's why it's called 'Sweetberry's,' hon." Dominique's warm laugh soothed Piper's heart.

"I love you, Dominique," Piper said. Her eyes filled with tears, and she turned away from the counter.

"Oh, now you come here." Dominique stepped out and wrapped Piper in a hug. "You okay?"

Piper nodded her head against Dominique's shoulder. "You smell good," she whispered.

Dominique laughed and squeezed Piper. "You're gonna be fine, lamb. Keep your chin up and trust Jesus. Can you do that for me?" Dominique dabbed at Piper's cheek.

"Yes, ma'am—I can do that." Piper smiled. "I'd love to stay and talk, but Trefor and Rosie will stop by in a couple of minutes. I need to get home."

"Hurry on then. Don't want that coffee gettin' cold." Dominique shooed her to the door. "Stop in next week. I'm baking beignets with cranberry powdered sugar."

"Stop," Piper said. "Seriously, Dominique, I can't keep stuffing my face."

Dominique grinned. "Desperate times call for desperate measures—or desperate snacks."

"I appreciate you, Dominique!" Piper called from the door.

"You too, baby! You too! Now get a move on!"

Piper turned into her Ferry Crossing neighborhood and scanned the road for reporters. After the radio announcement, she expected a few camped out at the end of her driveway. "Two?" she whispered. "You guys are slacking today." She parked near her garage and ran to the back door, where Trefor and Rosie waited.

"You made it through the wolves, huh? Why are they back?" Rosie asked.

Trefor grabbed his coffee from Piper and sipped. "Perfect—thanks."

"Hope you weren't waiting long." Piper said as she unlocked the back door.

"A couple minutes. I don't know how long Rosie was here."

"Two minutes longer than Trefor. So why are the reporters back?" Rosie asked.

"You didn't hear the announcement on the radio?"

Trefor and Rosie shook their heads.

"You know I listen to the Appleton station. They don't share Cranberry Harbor news. What's up?" Rosie asked.

"The police took Chase in for questioning. He's a suspect." Piper sighed. The weight of the past week threatened to suck her into a pit of despair. She took a deep breath. "It's so awful. I will not believe anyone I know murdered Daniel, much less my brother."

"Wow, that's hard, Piper. I'm sorry," Trefor said. He sat his coffee on the counter and pulled out his bottle of hand sanitizer. He rubbed the liquid across his hands and winced.

Piper frowned and said, "That cut hasn't healed yet? Let me see." She reached to grab Trefor's hand, but he turned to Rosie when she snatched the hand sanitizer from his hand.

"Phew, that's some strong stuff. Where did you get this?" She scrunched up her face and plugged her nose.

Trefor snatched the bottle and stuffed it into his pocket, glaring at Rosie. "My last trip to Mexico. I use the heavy-duty stuff for germs because I spend my time with kids, Rosie. They're germ factories."

Piper laughed. "He has a point. Maybe I should start a hand sanitizer habit."

Trefor nodded. "You can't take too many precautions, Piper."

Rosie cleared her throat and said, "Back to Chase."

"I don't know anything other than after our Core meeting, Lenny took Chase to the police. I expect a call and another meeting sometime today or tomorrow, but I've not heard anything since I left my parents' house," Piper said. She unwrapped the brownies from Dominique and inhaled.

"Wow, I don't eat chocolate, and those look amazing," Rosie said. She picked at the edge of a brownie and tasted a chunk. "Mmm . . . Dominque?"

Piper nodded. "She's practicing recipes for Cranberry Fest."

"That's months away," Trefor said.

"She's a perfectionist, and she's good at what she does. Plus, we benefit from tasting her practice runs. Have one." Piper pushed a brownie across the counter to Trefor.

"Sweetberry's bakery isn't vegan. Sorry. They smell amazing, though." He slide the brownie back to Piper.

"Oh!" Rosie yelled. "Lillie texted me after she called Quinn. Officer Hunky moved here six months ago from Milwaukee. He's thirty-eight, and he's single." Rosie waggled her eyebrows at Piper.

Piper turned away from Rosie to hide her grin and rinsed her hands. "Rosie," she said.

Rosie grinned and feigned innocence. "What? I'm passing on information. You're blushing. You're blushing, aren't you?"

"Wait a minute—who's 'Officer Hunky'?" Trefor asked.

"That gorgeous police chief handling the murder investigation," Rosie said.

"Hmm...," Trefor said. "I don't remember him." He stared at Piper.

Piper grabbed her brownie and took a bite. "Enough girl talk, Rosie." She bugged her eyes out at Rosie. "Let's sit for a few."

Rosie and Trefor followed her to the living room. "You always sit in the turret," Trefor said. "I've never been in here."

"The turret is my favorite sitting room, but I figured it's time to change things up a bit. Try a new room and see if it jiggles anything loose in our brains. Sit." Piper ordered.

Trefor and Rosie settled into the overstuffed chairs, and Piper curled up in the corner of the couch. "How was your class today, Trefor?"

"Three classes, all preschool." He shrugged. "I'm tired."

Piper and Rosie laughed. "You aren't kidding about the little ones," Rosie said. "When I teach preschool art at the academy,

I go home and soak my feet and snooze. Those little people are energetic—that's for sure."

"Any news other than Chase?" Piper asked and glanced at her phone. "No texts from my family yet. How long does questioning take anyway?"

"I don't know." Rosie shrugged. "Don't worry. Everything will work out. It has to."

"Have you heard anything around town, Trefor?" Piper asked. "People tell us they keep feeling watched from the shadows, but we don't have enough clues to piece the puzzle together."

"I haven't heard much other than that people worry. I don't know what's going on either. I believe the murder was random and that the murderer has left our area. Probably hit the highway immediately. Did the police ever release the time of death?" Trefor asked.

"That's why I'm frustrated, Trefor. They don't tell us anything, but my intuition says it's personal. I can't figure out why or who." Piper sighed.

Rosie paced and said, "Trefor has a point. Let's walk through the murder from a random horrible event angle." She grabbed the notebook. "Toss out some clues."

"The highway is close to Notes Music Centre," Trefor suggested.

"True," Piper said. "But Daniel didn't live in Cranberry Harbor. Why was he here?"

"There's no evidence he died here in Cranberry Harbor, is there?" Rosie asked.

"Not that I know of. So they killed Daniel and drug him into Notes?" Piper suggested.

"That back warehouse door—remember?" Trefor said.

Rosie pointed at Trefor and snapped her fingers. "Right! That opens onto the alley. Anyone can sneak in there."

"How does a random killer from who-knows-where know that information, though?" Piper asked.

"They cased the joint," Rosie said. "I never killed anyone; how do I know what runs through a demented mind?"

Piper sighed. "I know, but we have to throw out all angles. And how does a random killer randomly drag Daniel into the Notes warehouse and randomly stick him in my piano? No—it's too coincidental."

"The piano crates aren't labeled by name, though," Trefor said. "The crates stand in the order of delivery, and we have delivery notes with the serial number on the crate. Yours was closest to the door, so I can see what happened. He opened the door and opened the first crate."

"How do you know the murderer is a *he*?" Rosie shot the question at Trefor, her hands on her hips.

"I don't know. I'm just tossing out theories and ideas to help everyone. I'm not sure of anything," he said.

Piper rubbed her forehead and pinched the bridge of her nose. "*No one* is sure of anything right now, Trefor. No worries." She smiled and he nodded.

"Are we accomplishing anything here?" Rosie asked.

Piper sighed. "I'm not sure, but I appreciate you two sitting with me."

"Of course," Trefor said. "That's what friends do."

Rosie nodded. "Exactly. We're with you all the way, Piper. But I do have an appointment to pick up something, so I should skedaddle."

Piper raised her eyebrows. "What are you picking up?"

Rosie waved a finger at Piper. "That's for me to know and you to find out. I'll show ya soon." She grabbed her keys from her purse. "Oh, and Lisa keeps texting me, but I haven't answered yet."

Piper frowned, and Trefor glanced between them. "What's up with Lisa?" he asked.

"Nothing, other than she disappeared with the academy's fundraising money, and we haven't heard a word from her 'til today. She's texting as if nothing is weird, and she's coming to work on Monday."

Trefor adjusted the red beanie on his head and said, "Man, Lisa doesn't seem the type to take off with the money. Are you sure?"

"Nope. Not sure because she disappeared, and we've not seen or heard from her in days." Rosie said. "But she's also not the type to disappear for days either."

"I saw her last night," Piper said.

"You *what?*" Rosie screeched and plopped into her chair. "Why don't you tell me, girl? When? What happened? Where were you?"

"I drove out there," Piper said.

Rosie jumped to her feet. "What? When? Why? I mean, Piper, what were you thinking? Why didn't you call me? I don't want you alone when you do this stuff!" Rosie blew out a breath and slumped into the chair.

"Take it easy, Rosie. I got tired of sitting around here, so I drove to her house. I wanted to check if anything had changed. I followed a noise and found Lisa feeding her animals."

"That explains why they looked healthy. So Lisa comes at night and feeds them?" Rosie asked.

Piper shrugged. "I guess. When she saw me she said, 'You shouldn't be here, Piper!' Then she hopped into her car and peeled out of the driveway. I heard other noises and got spooked. So I left and then got pulled over for speeding."

Trefor laughed and said, "You? Miss 'Obey All the Rules' got pulled over for speeding?"

"Hey," Rosie said. "She got spooked. I don't blame her."

"Sorry," Trefor said.

"Who pulled you over?" Rosie asked. "Officer Hunky? Tell me Officer Hunky." Rosie's eyes twinkled, and she waggled her eyebrows at Piper.

"Chief Maxwell pulled me over, and when he found out where I had been, he yelled at me. He warned Lenny that he'll arrest me if I don't stay out of the investigation."

"Aha! It *was* Officer Hunky." Rosie laughed.

Piper held up her hand. "That's it—no more 'Officer Hunky.'"

Trefor stood and stretched. "I don't blame you for trying to solve this, Piper. I'd want to know too. I need to head out for the night. Be careful. I'm worried about you."

"Thanks, Trefor. Have a good night," Piper said. "Will you join us at church tomorrow?"

Trefor grimaced. "No, I uh . . . no."

"You're welcome to join us anytime," Piper said and smiled.

Trefor nodded and glanced away. "I might join you sometime."

Rosie stood. "I have to go too." She kissed Piper's cheek. "No more leaving the house at midnight chasing suspicions—got it?"

"I won't," Piper said. "But I need all of this to go away."

Rosie sighed. "Nancy Drew didn't have to work this hard."

Piper laughed and said, "Call me when you want to show me whatever you're picking up."

"I will. Toodles. See you at church."

Piper locked the doors and turned out the lights. Her dry eyes and aching body screamed for sleep. She climbed the stairs and sighed when she stepped on the stair tread that creaked and sagged. She rolled her eyes. "I love you old house, but you're about to turn me into a pauper. Every bit of you needs a rehab."

She sat on the side of her bed, gathering swirling phrases and clues. Her Bible sat on the side table opened to her favorite verses in Isaiah. Piper whispered a paraphrase, "You keep me in perfect peace because I trust you." She ran her fingers across the page. "Trust in the Lord forever: for in the Lord Jehovah is everlasting strength." She plopped her head onto the pillow and sighed, "I'm trying to trust, Lord, but my life seems out of control. I need some of your strength—because mine is gone."

Piper rolled over and closed her eyes, but her mind swirled. She glanced out her window at the moonlight and hummed a song from her childhood, "God Is Watching over Me."

The noisy old house creaked and groaned, and Piper's mind focused on every sound. A chill settled over her. She glanced around the dark room and at the window, expecting to see a creepy face peering through the glass.

She jumped out of bed. "You are two stories up, Piper, with nothing outside your window for anyone to use to peek at you. Go to sleep and stop worrying." She peeked out the window into her yard. Nothing.

She closed the shade and ran back to bed, diving under the sheet. Her heart pounded, and she rested her hand on her chest. "Piper Haydn, go to sleep." She reached out and grabbed her phone. "Music and sleep, or you're going to snooze through church."

The peaceful sounds of Debussy's "Petite Suite, En Bateau" filled the room. She closed her eyes and moved her fingers across the sheet. She played the piece in her mind until she drifted into a fitful sleep.

CHAPTER SIX

Sunday

When the alarm beeped, Piper groaned. She sat on the edge of her bed, holding back tears. "I did not sleep last night." She stretched and blew out a breath. "You're going to have to keep my eyes open today, God."

After a quick shower and two large mugs of steaming coffee, Piper hurried to dress for church. She grabbed her favorite red dress with the swirling skirt and a delicate white lace scarf her mom had knit for her.

She spun in front of the mirror and smiled as her skirt twirled. "Looking mighty fine for no sleep, Piper." She rolled her eyes and refilled her coffee mug before running to the car.

The reporters at the end of the driveway yelled when she backed onto the street, but she ignored their questions and drove through the crowd.

Piper pulled into the lot at Harbor View Bible Church and parked. A pleasant voice shouted, "Piper!"

She turned, and a reporter shoved a microphone in her face. "Is your brother in jail? Why did he kill Daniel Graves?"

Piper held up her hand and turned, hurrying into the church and ignoring the shouted questions. Rosie waited inside the foyer and grabbed her hand. "You're late. Why are you pale?" Rosie peeked out the front doors and scanned the parking lot. She frowned. "What happened?"

"Reporter out there." Piper frowned too. "I didn't say anything. They surprised me—that's all. I didn't sleep well last night." She sighed. "I'm fine. Let's go."

Rosie glared. "Should I karate chop 'em?"

"Well, since you don't know karate, that's not a great idea, Rosie. Plus, they'd report that a Haydn sent their friend to stop freedom of the press or something like that." She rolled her eyes. "Let it go. Come on. We'll have to sit in the front row if we walk in any later than we are right now."

Rosie shuddered. "I hate sitting up front."

"Because you have to pay attention." Piper teased.

"Hey."

Piper smiled, and they slid into the pew next to her mother right as the congregation was finishing the first hymn.

"Should we go to our class?" Rosie asked after the sermon.

Piper rolled her eyes. "What did you call the class? 'A bunch of losers going nowhere'? Why today?"

"We should try again." She pointed to the church bulletin. "The topic sounds interesting—'Sharing Your Faith in the Workplace.'"

"I suppose we can give the class another try." Piper smiled and kissed her mother goodbye. "I'll stop over for lunch, Mom."

Sarah Haydn nodded and waved goodbye to Rosie. "Perfect."

Piper and Rosie pushed through the crowd milling in the hallway. Friends stopped her. "We're praying," they said. Or they muttered, "Terrible."

Piper and Rosie dropped into chairs in their classroom. Piper sighed. "I'm exhausted. How many people stopped me?"

"Not sure," Rosie said. "At least you know they care."

"Piper and Rosie—you're back." The man at the front of the classroom smiled the cheesy smile of a used car salesman. His wide orange striped tie and brown polyester suit completed the look.

"Your topic sounds interesting, Nick. Thought we'd give it a try," Piper said.

Nick nodded, and the hair combed over his head slipped. "Such a terrible thing you're dealing with, Piper. I'm sorry. Is there any progress in the case?"

"She's not at liberty to share details." A familiar voice at the back of the room said.

Piper jerked her head in the direction of the voice. Chief Maxwell nodded and smiled.

Rosie nudged Piper and whispered, "What's *he* doing here?"

"I don't know," Piper said, frowning. "But he's giving me the creeps. Why did he follow me to church?"

Rosie grimaced and whispered, "If he's following you, you must be a suspect."

Piper's stomach lurched, and the rest of the class passed in a blur. She struggled to listen to Nick and learn from the teaching, but her mind raced.

Chief Maxwell tapped her shoulder after class. "Miss Haydn, Miss Hale." He nodded.

"What are you doing here?" Rosie asked. "It's bad enough that Piper has to deal with this mess everywhere else in her life. She should be free from dealing with this at church." She hissed, and her eyes bulged.

"Whoa, Miss Hale!" He held up his hand. "I didn't follow anyone to church."

"Then what are you doing here?" Piper asked, "If I'm not a suspect, you need to leave me alone, especially in my house of worship." She raised her chin and stared at him.

"Ladies, you misunderstand."

Nick stepped into the group and rested his arm around Chief Maxwell's shoulders. "Have you ladies met, Will? He's our new assistant class leader. He's teaching 'The Life of Christ' next session."

Chief Maxwell raised his eyebrows while a grin spread across his face.

"You. You what? You . . . " Piper spluttered, and heat rose in her cheeks.

"You don't get our emails?" Nick asked. "I told everyone about him months ago."

Piper's face flushed, and she turned on her heels and hurried from the room. When the sound of Chief Maxwell's chuckle floated down the hall, she clenched her jaw.

"That man is ridiculous," Rosie said.

Piper nodded and raced for the exit.

While driving to the Haydn home for lunch, Piper replayed the scene with the police chief. Her cheeks burned, and her heart pounded.

Why didn't I see him at church before? I'm there every Sunday.

Harbor View Bible Church was a large church, but Piper prided herself on knowing people. She introduced herself to newcomers all the time.

How did he become a regular attendee and I didn't notice? I need to stop taking pride in my friendliness at church. Isn't pride one of the seven deadly sins?

Piper hit the steering wheel and gritted her teeth. She was ready for life to resume the slow, sweet, charming pace she loved. Cranberry Harbor, her family, and her friends needed this case solved.

What's taking so long?

She parked under the sprawling oak tree in her parent's front lawn and hopped out. She stood for a moment gazing at the peaceful surroundings. Although she lived in her own house, the Haydn estate was home. So many happy memories of softball games on the front lawn, water balloon fights, and building snowmen in the frosty air. When red noses sent them inside to warm up, Mother served hot chocolate with fluffy marshmallows. They sat together in the warm kitchen, chattering about their plans to build the biggest snowman in town. Piper smiled at the happy memories. She loved her childhood and knew her parents had worked hard to give them a strong foundation.

Chase zipped into the driveway and parked his blue metallic Tesla next to her. He jumped out and sauntered over. "Hey, sis—whatcha doing out here?"

Piper grabbed him in a bear hug. "Reminiscing. How are you? What happened?"

Chase squeezed her back and shrugged. "Nothing. They asked a bunch of questions. I'm fine."

Piper frowned. "Why did they bring you in? I don't understand."

Chase glanced away. "It's nothing. Let's see what Mom made for lunch. I'm starving." He pointed at the side yard. "Remember when we played tackle football over there?" He chuckled. "I didn't expect to get my tooth knocked out by my prissy sister."

"Hey," Piper said. "I wasn't prissy back then. And if I remember correctly, you chose to be on the Bears. You deserved anything that happened to you. I invited you to join me on the Packers."

"'Go, Pack, go,' and all that, huh?" Chase laughed. "I was never much for wearing cheese on my head."

Piper nudged him with her elbow, "Well, you should try it sometime. Rosie says it's marvelous."

Chase laughed. "You're a nut."

"But you love me anyway," Piper smiled. She winked at her brother, but alarm bells rang at the way he brushed off her questions.

What are you keeping from me, Chase?

Chase held the front door open for her and followed her to the dining room. Their mother walked in carrying bowls of vegetables. "You're here. Cook outdid herself with this meal. She made roast and your favorite mashed potatoes, Chase." She gave each of them a kiss on the cheek and smiled. "Piper, I noticed you wore the scarf I knit for you."

Piper rolled the edge of the soft scarf between her fingers. "I love it, Mom. Thank you."

"That scarf took me an entire trip to Europe and back to knit. Be nice to it. I gave you washing instructions, right?"

Piper rolled her eyes. "Yes, Mother. I must handle anything you ever knit for me in a manner befitting a national treasure."

Sarah laughed. "I do believe you're exaggerating, my sweet daughter, but yes. Be gentle."

Braden and Emily sat on one side of the table, Asher and Landon on either side. "Auntie Piper, I won my game yesterday," Landon said. His toothless grin lit up the room.

"Awesome, Buddy. I'm sorry I couldn't come." Piper smiled at her nephew and blew a kiss to Asher. He squealed and hit the high chair tray. "Should we have an Auntie Piper day soon and have some fun?"

Landon smiled. "Yes, please, Aunt Piper."

"I'm quite busy right now, but I'll set up a plan with your mama in the next week or so."

Landon nodded and grinned.

"Are you practicing your piano lessons?" She raised her eyebrows.

"Yes, ma'am. Mama makes me practice every day. I played 'Old MacDonald Had a Farm' without looking at the page yesterday."

"Wow!" Piper said and gave him a thumbs-up. "Your granny made me practice every day too."

"Watch who you're calling 'Granny,' young lady." Sarah Haydn glared at Piper, but her eyes twinkled. "'Granny' is for old women, and I'm quite young. I believe they should call me 'Glammy.'"

"You are glamorous indeed, Sarah." Jack Haydn entered the room and kissed Sarah on the cheek. "But that sounds rather hipster if you ask me." He winked at his family gathered around the table.

"I saw a 'Glammy' T-shirt," Sarah said. "You should sell them at the orchard store, Jack." Sarah laughed. "I'd buy one."

"Do they have a 'Glampy' shirt for Dad?" Piper chuckled.

Jack grinned. "Let's pray," he said. The group bowed their heads. "Dear Father, we thank you for our blessings. I am thankful to have my children and grandchildren gathered around my table today. Thank you for the sermon at church this morning and the freedom to worship you together. Bless cook for preparing this food, and thank you for providing for us."

Amens echoed around the table, and one-year-old Asher yelled, "Eat!"

Emily laughed. "He's learned that 'Amen' means food." She blew the toddler a kiss, and everyone chuckled.

Piper glanced around the table at her family. A swell of gratitude bubbled in her heart. This home, these people, the laughter, and the familiar aroma of Sunday dinner served as a balm for her exhausted soul. A tear slid down her cheek, and she grabbed her napkin to dab it away.

She glanced up and found her dad staring. He frowned, but she smiled and grabbed her fork. He turned to Emily. "How are you and my new grandbaby feeling today, Emily?"

"I'm fine, Glampy." She grinned. "Thanks for asking."

Chatter and the sounds of a pleasant family dinner filled the dining room, but Piper sensed tension. Chase didn't enter the conversation, and her father's frown and his glances around the table unnerved her.

"Chase, any news?" Braden asked.

Chase mumbled, but Dad said, "Not at dinner. Lenny will stop over to update us at two. Until then, we are enjoying a pleasant meal together." He glanced around the table, stopping at each person until he or she nodded in agreement. Classic Dad. He ruled the family with a look or word, and everyone toed the line. Piper bristled at Dad's rules as a child, but she realized as she grew older that he wanted the best for them. He never yelled or manipulated them, but they were Haydns, and along with the name came responsibility and expectations.

Braden glanced at his watch. "Can Emily lay Asher down for a nap before Lenny arrives, Mom? We'll all pay the price if he doesn't get his nap." He rolled his eyes but grinned at his baby boy.

"My grandbaby isn't capable of behaving like a bear—are you now, sweet little Asher?" Sarah baby-talked across the table, and Asher waved his spoon and squealed.

Jack raised his eyebrows and blew out a breath. "Let's all help Mother clean up. We'll meet in the library after Emily gets Asher down for his nap."

The Haydns nodded and jumped to clear the table. Piper grabbed empty plates and hurried to the kitchen. At the door she glanced back at the table. Chase stared out the window, and tears rolled down his cheeks. Her stomach twisted, and a chill settled over her heart.

Something is very wrong.

Piper filled the time between kitchen clean-up and the meeting of The Core by playing the piano. She rested her fingers on the keyboard and glanced around the conservatory—her favorite room in the Haydn mansion. The sunlight streamed through the windows, and Piper considered curling up in the chair by the window to sleep. But a nap might leave her groggy, and playing the piano energized her soul.

The acoustics in the conservatory produced incredible sound when Piper pounded out the furious pieces—Beethoven's "Coriolan Overture" and Rachmaninoff's "The Bells." But she chose hymns for her Sunday stress relief session. She played with her eyes closed, pouring out her pain and confusion to God. The music soothed her soul, and she smiled at the sunshine pouring through the windows. The question of who murdered Daniel and the worry about Chase didn't change, but her heart relaxed.

Okay, God. I will trust you to get us through this.

She played the "Flight of the Bumblebee" for fun. Her fingers grazed the keyboard as she played. A smile spread across her face and a laugh bubbled inside. She played the final notes and closed the lid over the keyboard.

"Bravo!" Emily said, plopping into the chair by the window. "Piper, you play so lovely. I didn't even see your hands moving when you played—like Schroeder in the *Peanuts* cartoon." She laughed. "I wish my parents hadn't let me quit lessons." She rolled her eyes. "But I whined and begged until they gave in." She stretched her legs onto the ottoman. "Not making that mistake with Landon."

Piper smiled. "I didn't know you came in. Is Asher sleeping already?"

"Braden offered to lay him down, and I didn't refuse."

"Do you want a blanket or some tea?" Piper asked.

Emily laughed and shifted in the chair, crossing her ankles. "I'm pregnant, Piper. I'm not fragile. But I did need to get these feet up for a bit. Thank you for the private concert. I'd listen to you play all day."

"Thank you, Emily. Playing helps me—in here." She rested her hand on her heart. "I can't explain why, but I'm thankful."

"How are you? Really?" Emily asked. "I'm so worried about you."

Piper sighed. "I don't know, Emily. Sometimes I'm handling everything, and sometimes I'm in the depths of despair. I'm trying to trust that God has a plan and that He's working this out, but . . ." She trailed off. "How's Braden?"

"I'd say he's the same, but you know Haydn men don't talk about their feelings."

Piper nodded and rolled her eyes.

Emily giggled. "He's concerned for you and Chase, of course. He's worried about the impact on the orchard and town. He's worried that they won't solve the murder and that this cloud of suspicion won't go away."

"It's hard. I can't even believe it. We live in Cranberry Harbor, for goodness' sake," Piper said.

"Cranberry Harbor doesn't need any of this—I agree. But we aren't insulated from real-world problems here. It seems we should be with all the charm and small-town friendliness."

"Is Braden convinced they won't solve Daniel's murder?" Piper asked.

Emily blew out a breath. "I wouldn't say 'convinced'—*worried.*"

"There you are, girls." Sarah Haydn breezed in and sat across from Piper. She pushed her hair back from her face and sighed. "I . . ." She turned away and rested her chin on her hand, staring out the window.

"I'm sorry, Mom," Piper said. "Do you have any idea what Lenny's going to say?"

Sarah twisted her wedding ring around her finger. She wiped a tear from her eyes and smiled. "Everything will work out exactly as it's supposed to." Her voice was a little too cheerful.

Emily glanced at her watch. "Ten minutes. Should we move to the library? And no comments about my pregnant waddle." She giggled, and Sarah hugged her.

"You have a beautiful little waddle, sweetheart. I, on the other hand, was a train wreck. Chase was the worst—he was huge." She swallowed and hurried faster down the hall. Piper jogged to keep up with her mom.

"Ladies," Lenny said.

Piper nodded. "What did you learn?"

"I'll share when everyone gathers," Lenny said, shuffling papers and closing his briefcase.

Piper blew out a breath to ease the stress rising in her back. Her stiff shoulders ached. She needed a nap.

Braden and Jack slid into their spots, followed by Chase, who kept his head down and mumbled when Piper greeted him.

Jack cleared his throat. "Lenny, what have you heard?"

Lenny adjusted his glasses and glanced around the room. He read from his notes. "The Cranberry Harbor Police Department brought Chase in for questioning regarding the murder of Daniel Graves. Chase answered every question I allowed, and they considered him cooperative with authorities. Their main suspicion came after an investigation in Daniel's financial affairs when several payments to one C. Haydn came to light." Lenny glanced around the room and cleared his throat. "After questioning, Chase admitted he received several payments from the deceased for the dispersal of illegal substances."

Piper gasped and stared at the top of Chase's head. His head bent further toward his chest, and he sighed.

"What?" Jack Haydn stood and hit the table with his fist. "Chase!"

Piper's hands shook, and she shivered. "Chase?" She asked in a low voice. "Did you know Daniel sold drugs when I was dating him?" She clenched her teeth, holding the torrent of angry words threatening to burst out.

I love Chase, but if I find out he knew Daniel sold drugs and let me go to the altar to marry him, I will pummel my brother.

"No, Piper. I promise. I wouldn't have let you get that far if I knew." He raised his hands. "I found out later. I only helped him a couple times."

"A couple times?" Sarah said, her face pale and her cheeks flushed.

"If you need money, Chase, I have work available. You aren't poor. Why on earth did you sell drugs?" Jack Haydn's voice thundered.

Chase raised his chin and stared at his father. "I wanted to do my own thing, Dad. Be my own person—all that."

Braden raised his eyebrows. "But you're *not* your own person, Chase. You are a Haydn, and we have a reputation to uphold and a town to watch out for. If you want to do your own thing, you open a business apart from the orchard, Chase. You don't sell drugs." His voice rose, and he emphasized every word.

Chase jumped from his chair, eyes blazing. "Oh, I know I'm a Haydn, Braden." He spit out the words and turned from the table. He made it to the door before Jack's calm voice stopped him.

"Chase Haydn, sit down. Right now. You are dealing with a horrible mess, and you're not going anywhere until this meeting is over. Do you understand me?" His eyes were hard, and his jaw clenched. He pointed to Chase's chair at the end of the table. "I said, 'Sit.'"

Chase stared for a moment, his Adam's apple bobbing up and down when he swallowed. He returned to his chair and said, "Yes, sir." He didn't return willingly, and anger simmered under his calm exterior. But Piper knew Chase and his tone of voice.

Jack glanced at Lenny. "What else? Because selling pot isn't the same as murder."

Lenny grabbed the paper. "The sale wasn't pot, and Chase is to stay in town for further questioning. Daniel refused to pay Chase for the final delivery, and Chase threatened him. One of Daniel's associates heard and in hindsight reported to the police Chase's threat."

Everyone turned to Chase, who stared at his feet.

"Son," Jack Haydn said. "Did you murder Daniel Graves?"

The color drained from Chase's face. "No!" His voice croaked, reminding Piper of a frog.

Frogs. Ugh.

Lenny cleared his throat, "The cause of death is released."

Piper's head snapped back to Lenny. Her stomach twisted, and Daniel's lifeless face in her Steinway flashed through her mind.

"Daniel Graves was strangled with a thin metal object—possibly a wire. The crime lab in Madison found ligature marks on his neck and an odd substance." He shuffled through the papers and adjusted his glasses. "Traces of methanol and aloe."

Piper frowned. "What in the world?" She whispered and glanced around the table. Her family stared at one another.

Piper's stomach rolled, and she bolted from the room.

"I'm gonna be sick."

Sarah Haydn tucked Piper into her childhood bed and kissed her forehead. "Take a nap, sweetheart. Life will seem better after you rest." She tiptoed out, and Piper drifted into a fitful sleep.

When she opened her eyes in the dark room, she peeked at the clock on the nightstand.

"Seven o'clock? My goodness!" She sat up and grabbed her phone, scrolling through messages—several from Rosie.

----**Spending time with my mom tonight. I have something to show you tomorrow. See you.**

----**You're gonna love it.**

Still no text or email from Lisa. Piper frowned.

Why did she message Rosie and not me? Rosie's not her boss.

**--Hey, you busy tonight? I wanted to see how you're doing. I
can bring chocolate.**

"Bless your Birkenstock loving heart, Trefor." She smiled and
replied.

--Absolutely. Give me an hour, please.

--K

Piper pulled the quilt over the bed and smoothed the wrinkles.
She glanced around her room, and a pang of nostalgia twisted her
heart. "I miss life as a carefree little girl sometimes." She ran her
hand over the white dresser with a secret drawer she had begged for
when she turned ten. She popped open the panel and reached in
for her diary. She flipped pages and stopped at a page titled "What
I want to do when I grow up." In her middle school handwriting, a
long list followed—every *i* dotted with a puffy heart. She ran her
finger down the list, reading silently until she reached the last two.
"I want to be a mom of twelve children and a piano teacher."

Piper laughed. "Oh, young Piper, old Piper has the piano teacher
down, but she can't handle twelve children. How about two? If I
ever find someone, that is." She sighed and pushed the diary into
the secret compartment.

She would say goodbye to her parents and get home before Trefor
stopped by with her chocolate.

She hurried through the house, but her parents weren't home. She
scribbled a note and stuck it to the refrigerator. When she stepped
outside, Chase's Tesla was gone.

"Chase, we love you, you know," she whispered to the empty yard
and slid behind the wheel of her car. Piper flipped through radio
channels and stopped when Wisconsin Public Radio played the
pleasant sounds of a symphony. She took a deep breath and turned
the car toward home.

When Piper pulled into her driveway, she thought Trefor was sitting in the dark on the porch swing. She checked the road—no car. "Hmm . . . he doesn't usually walk over here." She hurried onto the porch, and the motion light flipped on. Instead of Trefor, a massive stuffed frog with a red ribbon around the neck sat on the swing. Piper frowned and hurried inside, leaving the frog behind.

"I need to install security cameras. Should have done that months ago. I'm getting quite sick of the random frog appearances," she said to the empty house and ran around switching on the lights. "Maybe Rosie's right. I need to call the chief about this."

She turned the fire on under her tea kettle to brew some of Maisy's relaxing tea. The Haydn Music Academy was reopening tomorrow, and she needed a good night's rest. She leaned on the counter listening for the tea kettle's whistle and ran through the list of things she needed to accomplish. She hoped most of her students would show up ready to learn tomorrow, but she would understand if they didn't.

The murder isn't solved, and I'm not in the clear. My brother is a suspect, and everything is up in the air.

"Nope, I don't blame any parent who removes his or her child after all this. I just hope I can keep the academy open."

A knock at the kitchen door broke her musings. Trefor stood peering in and waving.

"Trefor, you made it."

"Of course I did," he said. "Chocolate." He handed her a to-go box with a slice of chocolate pie.

"Oh, my, Trefor—that looks amazing." She grabbed a fork and dug into the dessert. "Mmm."

Trefor smiled and adjusted his red beanie. His long hair escaped from the front of the hat, and he pushed it back from his face.

"Where did you find that shirt?" Piper asked, pointing at his rainbow-colored shirt.

"Rosie mentioned she saw it at the thrift store the other day. Perfect, isn't it?" He smiled.

"Show me the socks," Piper said.

Trefor pulled up a leg of his skinny jeans and stuck out his foot. "Ninja Turtles," he said.

Piper smiled. "You do find the craziest stuff. What did you do today? Missed you at church."

Trefor rolled his eyes. "Told you I don't really do church anymore."

"One of these days I'll butter you up, and you'll say yes." Piper smiled at Trefor and grabbed her mug. "Want some tea?"

He waved his hand. "No thanks."

Piper frowned at the flash of red on his palm. "Is your hand still hurt from that paper cut?"

Trefor shoved his hand in his pockets. "I'm fine. Does the academy open tomorrow? What's the plan?"

"I'm planning for a normal day full of classes, but I don't know what the parents are planning. I don't blame them for waiting 'til life settles down or leaving altogether. I hope they don't, but . . ." Piper sighed.

Trefor nodded. "I understand. So hard. Well, I'll send my best thoughts that tomorrow goes well for you."

"Thanks. Let's sit. My feet hurt," Piper said. Piper plopped onto the sofa and pointed to the piano. "Play me a tune, Trefor."

"No. Not in front of you. I'd die of embarrassment."

Piper laughed. "Oh, come on. You're a music teacher too. What do you enjoy playing?"

"The guitar."

"I meant on the piano, silly." Piper tossed a pillow at him, and he caught it. He smiled, but Piper turned away at the look in his eyes. *I'm not interested, Trefor.*

Trefor smiled. "You play something for me. I don't ever get to hear you play." He leaned back on the couch and pointed to the piano.

Piper moved to the piano bench and played a movement from "Claire de Lune." She frowned at the twang from the high C but turned to Trefor and bowed.

"Bravo!" He clapped.

"I have to get the piano tuned. The C is making an odd sound." She frowned.

Trefor pulled out his hand sanitizer and slathered his hands. He winced when the sanitizer touched his sore.

"Trefor, let me see your hand. That paper cut shouldn't bother you so much. When did it happen?"

He shook his head. "I'm fine. It's almost better."

Piper glanced at the clock on the wall—bedtime. Big day tomorrow. She sniffed the air. "What's in that stuff, Trefor? It's so strong."

He pulled the bottle out and read the ingredients list. "Water, isopropyl alcohol, aloe, a bunch of other stuff, glycerin, methanol. That's a mouthful." He glanced up and smiled. "I get it in Mexico 'cause the FDA banned it for some reason. Only kind that works for me. Why?"

"No reason. I was curious. Like I said, it's strong." Something niggled in the back of her brain, sounding an alarm bell, but she couldn't figure out why.

Trefor stood and stretched. The scent of his hand sanitizer enveloped her. "I should leave—getting late," he said.

A scene from the music store warehouse flashed through Piper's mind—Trefor's work table lined with hand sanitizer bottles and piano wire. Had she seen a green frog on his work table? She blinked. She shook her head to clear cobwebs.

"What?" Trefor asked, his eyes narrowing.

"Have you . . .? Did you . . .?" Piper rubbed the space between her eyebrows.

"Have I what?" Trefor asked.

"Have you left me frogs everywhere?"

His face lit up, and he nodded. "I thought you didn't notice. I wanted to give them to you because Debussy had a green frog to help him write music." He waved his hands. "I thought they might help you."

Piper stared at him for a moment, the niggling in her brain screeching at her to let Trefor leave. Instead, she said, "But Trefor, they were inside my house and my locked music academy. How did you get in?"

Trefor raised his chin and stared down his nose. "I have ways."

She frowned. "Coming into my house without permission is wrong, Trefor. What were you thinking?" She shivered as a cold chill ran up her spine. Lenny's words from the meeting of The Core rang in her mind.

"Daniel Graves was strangled with a thin metal object—possibly a wire. The crime lab in Madison found ligature marks on his neck and an odd substance. Traces of methanol and aloe."

Her eyes widened, and she stepped away from Trefor.

Methanol and aloe, the cut on his hand. Piano wire.

"What?" Trefor asked, stepping close to Piper.

She took a deep breath. "Nothing. I need to get ready for bed, Trefor." Her voice trembled, and she cleared her throat to cover the sound.

His eyes narrowed, and his nostrils flared. He stepped closer to Piper, trapping her against the piano. "What's going on, Piper?" he asked, glaring down at her. "Why are you backing away from me?"

Piper's hands trembled, and she squeezed her eyes shut. The corner of the piano lid pressed into her back. "Nothing, Trefor.

Nothing at all. I'm tired—long week." Her voice dropped to a whisper. "Please—you're scaring me." She whimpered.

Trefor glanced around the room. He cleared his throat. "Piper, I'm um . . ."

"It's fine, Trefor. I'm tired and need to head to bed." Her voice quivered, and her knees gave out.

Trefor grabbed her, and his eyes hardened. "No, Piper—you're not going anywhere," he hissed in her ear. His fingers dug into her arm.

"Please, Trefor. You're hurting me," she whispered. "Let me go. I won't say a word." She planted a cheerful smile on her face. Her body tensed and she shuddered. She swallowed the tears threatening to spill down her cheeks.

The cords in Trefor's neck bulged, and he pointed a finger in Piper's face. When he laughed, the sound sent shivers up Piper's spine. "You won't say anything? What kind of idiot do you think I am? I'll walk out the door, and you'll call the police chief to come running. No. No one's going anywhere." His fingers tightened around her arm. "I did nothing but pay attention to you. I promoted your academy. I brought you chocolate. I listened to your sob stories when Daniel left you at the altar. I brought you those frogs." His voice rose into a screech.

"No, no—you're right, Trefor," Piper said, her voice calm despite the pounding heartbeat in her ears. "I know. I know."

"Don't patronize me, Piper. I asked you out how many times? And every time you said no. You didn't even give me a chance." His screech returned, and his eyes bugged out.

God, please help. I don't know what to do.

Piper's head swam, and spots floated in her eyes. "I should have listened to you. You're right. I'm sorry."

"Too late. It's too late. You had your chance." He tightened his grip on her arm, and she yelped. He reached into the piano and plucked out a wire from the high end of the keyboard.

Piper's eyes widened, and her stomach lurched when she gasped, "How? What?"

Trefor chuckled. "Every time I came over, I loosened the tuning pin. You never noticed a thing, did you?"

She raised her chin and stared at his eyes inches away from her. "I noticed."

"You didn't do anything about it. You never said thank you for the frogs, by the way." He stared down at her, his eyes hard.

She shivered.

"I took Rosie's notebook, too. Valuable information in there—thanks."

Piper's eyes narrowed, and she jerked to pull away from Trefor.

"No, no, no, Miss Haydn." His fingers dug further into her arm, and the blood pounded in her veins.

Tears stung her eyes, and her dry throat burned. "I couldn't say thank you for the frogs, Trefor. You never told me you snuck into my house and planted them. That's breaking and entering." She stared at him.

He laughed and gripped the piano wire. "You never cared about me, Piper. Everything is about you. You're a stuck-up rich kid who used me. You use Rosie too. You're disgusting." His voice rose to a high pitch, and his eyes darted around the turret room. He pulled her away from the piano, but she grabbed the edge. "Let go, Piper." He pulled, and she shook her head. Trefor reached and pushed the prop holding the cover of the piano up. The lid slammed onto Piper's fingers.

She screamed, and a wave of nausea rolled in her stomach. "Please, Trefor," she whispered. "Don't hurt me." Her fingers throbbed under the piano lid and bright lights blinked before her eyes.

"'Don't hurt me,'" he mocked. "Daniel said the same thing." A chuckle escaped Trefor's throat, and Piper shivered.

"Why did you kill him?" Piper whispered and gritted her teeth, holding back nausea. Her fingers numbed.

Trefor's eyes widened, and he frowned. "Why did I kill him? Because he hurt you, Piper. I couldn't stand to see your sadness after what he did to you. I did it for you. You didn't deserve what he did to you." Trefor smoothed her hair over and over. She jerked her head away from his hand. "He answered my phone call that night, and I asked him to meet me at the warehouse. He remembered me. Know what he said to me?"

"No," Piper whispered.

"He said, 'Oh, you're the hipster idiot that won't leave Piper alone, aren't you?'" Trefor shouted. "Daniel was a jerk."

Piper nodded.

"You're no better, Piper. That's why I put him in your Steinway." Trefor chuckled a high cackle.

Piper trembled, and a headache pounded behind her eyes. She took a deep breath, "Trefor, it's all behind us. Now that Daniel's gone, I have more time to get to know you. I'm sorry I didn't let you know how much I appreciate you."

Trefor's grip tightened, and he stared into her eyes. Then he grabbed her arm, digging his fingers in. "You're messing with me, Piper. You just want me to let you go, and you'll call the police. You'll let me down, Piper. Everyone lets me down." Trefor paced behind her. Piper glanced at her reflection in the turret windows, wondering if she could pull away and run for the door.

He's too close.

Piper took a deep breath and attempted to pull her fingers out from under the piano lid. Trefor lunged.

Her voice shook, and she tried to remain calm. "All right, Trefor—I won't move. I'm standing right here." She leaned on the piano, her fingers throbbed, and her legs ached.

"Trefor, please let me go. I won't tell."

Trefor screamed a deep guttural scream and pulled Piper away from the piano, the lid pinching the tips of her fingers when he dragged her hands out of the closed piano.

She screamed again. "Trefor. Let me go! No!" She twisted and dropped to the floor, but Trefor grabbed her. He lifted the piano wire over her head, and she thrashed and pulled away.

He jerked her to the stairs. "Come with me, Piper, and no one gets hurt." The piano wire rested around her neck, and his fingers gripped her arm. Trefor pushed her to the stairs.

Oh, God—please help. I'm going to die.

Piper stifled a scream as Trefor shoved her to the stairs. She dropped to the floor, but the piano wire resting on her neck tightened. Trefor controlled her movements.

"Don't do that, Piper," he warned, pulling her to her feet. "I won't let go of the wire next time," he whispered. Piper's stomach lurched at his hot breath in her ear.

"Up," he said, pushing her onto the first step. "I did this for you, Piper. Everything I did was for you. But you don't appreciate my efforts. You only have eyes for that police officer."

"No, Trefor—that wasn't me. Rosie's the one. I never talked about him." Piper's voice trembled.

"I saw you look at him, Piper. I saw you. You never looked at *me* that way. You never made *me* part of your life. I tried so hard, Piper. So hard."

"Trefor," she whispered, "I invited you over here to talk and drink coffee almost every day."

Trefor laughed and gritted his teeth. "No, Piper. I invited myself over every day. I tried to make you notice me, but you're in your little rich girl world. You're so important, and I'm the lowly errand boy. It wasn't supposed to end this way." He pulled the wire, and Piper coughed.

Don't say 'end.'. . . No, it's not over. Keep him talking.

"I wanted you to come to church with me this morning, Trefor, didn't I?" she asked. Her mind raced, attempting to find something to soothe him.

Trefor laughed. Piper's chest tingled at the mirthless sound. Her hands shook, and the back of her throat ached.

"Please!" he shouted. "I am not your little Christian project, Piper! You never invited me to work for you. You never invited me home to meet Mommy and Daddy. You never even let me meet your brothers. Not even the druggie."

Piper stiffened. "He's not a druggie."

"Right? And I'm not a musician either." Trefor squeezed Piper's arm. "That's why he sat at the police station all day yesterday while I ran errands for the lovely Piper." He pushed her back, nudging her up the stairs.

I can't let him take me upstairs.

Piper didn't know Trefor's plan, but her instincts screamed, and she prepared to fight. She reached for the stair rail on the way up. If she slowed the progress up the stairs, maybe he would . . .

What? What do I think will happen? Nothing will happen. He's going to kill me.

Her eyes stung, and the lump in her throat hurt. Tears she tried to will away ran down her cheeks. Her shoulders slumped.

It's no use. No one can hear me, and I'm not strong enough to fight him. Not with my hands messed up.

When Trefor had slammed the piano lid on her fingers, she heard a crunch. Her fingers throbbed, and trying to grab the stair rails was an exercise in futility. Her mind raced to formulate a last-ditch plan. She glanced around, planning to bolt into her room at the top of the stairs and lock the door. But he would pull the piano wire into her neck if she ran.

She squeezed her eyes shut and tried to still her trembling hands. She shivered and gasped for air. "Trefor, please. Please let me go," she whimpered.

"'Oh, Trefor, please let me go,'" he mocked. His sing-song voice sent a wave of doubt through Piper.

I can't do this. I'm not strong enough or brave enough. God, please help me.

"No more stalling," he said, digging his finger into her bruised arm. Trefor pushed his arm into Piper's back.

The wire tightened with each step, and she leaned on the rail to catch her breath. She blinked, wanting to push away the blackness swimming in front of her eyes and the white lights twinkling across her eyelids. She gulped for air and fought nausea roiling in her stomach.

I'm so tired. I can't do this.

Her muscles screamed, and she wanted to sit down. Confusion swirled in her mind as she struggled to move up the stairs. Trefor dug into her arm, pushing her with his body.

"You were my friend." She gasped. "I trusted you."

"I was never your friend, Piper. You and I both know that. I was only a convenient way to get your coffee in the morning. I see that now. Don't try to fool me. You're trying to get out of what you deserve." The monotone inflection in Trefor's voice chilled Piper. She shivered, and her teeth chattered.

Piper reached the top step, and Trefor pushed her from behind.

It's now or never.

Piper grasped the newel at the top of the stair rail and gritted her teeth as pain from her injured fingers shot up her arm. She held tight as Trefor pushed, but she remained planted at the top of the stairs.

Piper shook, and her clammy hands slipped when Trefor leaned against her back. He pulled the piano wire tight, and Piper's last-ditch plan came together. She pushed with all her might against the post and fell back onto Trefor.

He screamed and grabbed Piper as they tumbled down the stairs. She smiled.

I didn't let him kill me without a fight.

Piper heard a yell and a scream. Her head slammed into the wall, and she landed in a heap at the bottom of the stairs.

CHAPTER SEVEN

Monday

P iper smiled and sat on the piano bench, resting her fingers on the smooth keys of her new Steinway. She adjusted her music book and gave her fingers a quick stretch. She turned to the auditorium and smiled, bowing her head in a slight nod, and played a selection from her favorite Debussy piece "Douze Etudes."

Her fingers glided over the keyboard in a whirlwind. The audience sat in silence, mesmerized by her grace. The melody filled the auditorium, and Piper's heart sang. The recital had gone off without a hitch, every student's piece played to perfection. The Steinway added a level of legitimacy to her piano studio. Filled with pride for her accomplishments, Piper finished playing and stood to the roaring cheers of students and parents.

Lights reflected off the shiny black piano, and Piper bowed. The loud applause and cheers echoed in her ears. She smiled and rested her hand on her heart, then bowed again. Cries of "Encore! Encore!" filled the room, and Piper smiled.

Trefor stepped onto the stage and joined her in a bow. Piper frowned.

What's he *doing here?*

Trefor rested his hand on her back and pulled her close—too close. Piper pulled away, but Trefor leaned in and whispered, "Let's play the duet." He held her hand and led her to the piano, and they played "Petit Suite" together. Piper glanced at Trefor, confused, but continued playing.

We didn't practice this. It's not on the schedule.

She hadn't played duets since Juilliard, so she closed her eyes and played from memory—every note flawless, every tone perfection. She took a deep breath, enjoying the peace flooding her heart.

She smiled and opened her eyes. Daniel Graves' gray, lifeless face peered at her from the side of the music stand. She jumped off the piano bench and stood screaming and pointing. The auditorium exploded into a chaotic frenzy.

Trefor exploded into a demented laugh and played while Piper shivered. She frowned at Trefor's happiness. She pointed and screamed until the pain in her throat silenced the sound.

She collapsed into a heap on the floor, her black gauzy skirt floating into a circle around her crumpled body. The black scarf tied at her neck tightened, and Piper gasped for air. Her heart pounded, and the noise in the auditorium dimmed.

Why does my throat hurt?

Piper moved her head from side to side and grabbed her throat. A hand grabbed hers, and she screamed.

"Piper. You're safe, Piper. Lie still."

Piper tried to open her eyes, but her eyelids weighed a thousand pounds. She swallowed and grimaced. "Hurts," she croaked.

Piper squeezed her eyes shut. The bright light hurt. She needed to ask Don to install lights with less wattage because the light glared on her music, and the notes waved. She opened her eyes, and the bright light blurred her vision.

"Hey, Piper—I saw you open your eyes. Can you try that again? Let me see your pretty eyes."

Piper frowned. She didn't recognize the voice.

Why do they interrupt my playing? How did they get on stage?

She sighed. After the recital she would figure out a way to keep people off the platform during a performance. After finishing this piece, she would write a strongly worded email or lecture the audience.

The voice interrupted her wandering mind, and someone grabbed her shoulder. "Piper, open your eyes."

She opened her eyes and squinted at the bright light. The pain in her throat stopped her from screaming. Faces peered down, and she scanned the crowd, breathing a sigh of relief when Daniel's gray, lifeless face didn't stare back at her. She frowned.

One of the voices above her chuckled. "She's awake. Look at that frown. Piper, can you hear me?"

She frowned and nodded.

"You're in the hospital, honey." A woman's voice said. "We're gonna take real good care of you." A hand patted her arm, and she flinched. "I'm sorry, sweetie. I didn't mean to scare you. I'm Angela, your nurse. I'll be here for you whatever you need."

"How many fingers am I holding up?" the other voice said.

Piper squinted and frowned. "Five?" She croaked around the pain in her throat. "What?"

"Touch my fingers."

Piper reached and tapped the fingers in front of her. She blew out a breath and frowned.

"Touch your nose."

Piper touched her nose and shifted her head away from the light.

"Stay with me, Piper. What day is it?" the voice said.

Piper sighed and closed her eyes. "Sunday," she whispered.

"Don't worry about anything right now, Piper. Rest," the voice said as someone patted her arm and adjusted the blanket.

The voices softened, and Piper drifted back to sleep.

I'm so tired.

Piper's eyes fluttered open, and she stared at the ceiling. She frowned and tried to gather her thoughts. They flitted about like marbles falling through a laundry basket. She sighed and closed her eyes. *Where am I?*

"Oh, you're awake," a deep voice said.

Piper's turned in the direction of the voice, willing her foggy vision to clear. Several moments passed before Piper recognized the out-of-uniform police chief. He sat in a chair in the corner of the room wearing jeans and a blue striped button-down shirt open at the collar. He jumped from the chair and walked to the bedside.

"Where am I?" Piper croaked.

"Harbor General. Do you remember what happened last night?" His gentle voice soothed her frayed nerves.

Piper frowned. "The hospital?"

"Yes, ma'am. Nothing?"

"Trefor," Piper croaked again and touched her neck. "Throat hurts."

"I'm sorry, Miss Haydn." Chief Maxwell grabbed the water on her side table and handed it to her, but she grimaced, attempting to hold the handle. "Oh, sorry. Here." He pushed the button on her bed to raise her head and held the straw to her mouth.

She frowned.

"Take a drink," he said and smiled. He raised his eyebrows and pointed to the cup, encouraging her as she did with her baby nephew.

Piper took a long sip and grimaced when the cold water ran down her raw throat. She held up her hand and nodded.

Chief Maxwell set the cup back down and patted her arm. "Can I help with anything else? Bed up or down? Are you hungry?"

Piper gazed into his eyes and saw kindness but something else she didn't want to see. She turned away.

A nurse bustled in and set a tray onto Piper's bedside table. "Jell-O, juice, and applesauce for you, my dear. What can I interest you in this morning?" She turned to Chief Maxwell. "Sir, how long do you plan to stay?" She rested her hands on her hips and stared.

"Until she can answer questions, I'm the only one who can wait in this room." He smiled.

The nurse turned to Piper. "Are you feeling strong enough? Your mama wants in, and there's a mob of people in the waiting room asking after you."

Piper smiled. "I'll try," she whispered in a gravelly voice.

"Good, baby. You can do it." She turned on the chief and pointed in his face. "This girl needs her rest, so hurry up and get out of here. Understand?" She stared, and Chief Maxwell nodded.

When the nurse left, he stepped to her bed. "What do you want to eat?" he asked.

Piper pointed to the applesauce cup. He opened the foil and set a spoon into the container. Piper reached for the spoon with her bandaged hands and dribbled applesauce on her gown.

"Oh, sorry," he said and picked up the container. He dipped the spoon in and held it to Piper's lips.

She blushed but opened her mouth, and he smiled and nodded. He helped her eat a few spoonfuls of applesauce, whispering encouragements. "You can do it. Good girl. There ya go."

Piper wanted to feed herself, but his smile and encouraging words washed over her, and she accepted his help.

Oh, my—those brown eyes.

Piper smiled and waved her hand.

"Done? You didn't eat much." He frowned. "One more bite?" He waggled his eyebrows and flashed a cheesy smile.

Tiny gray hairs curled at his temple, and laugh lines around his eyes caught Piper's attention. Heat rose in her cheeks at the questions swirling in her fuzzy brain—not police officer questions either.

Oh, goodness—he's handsome.

She waved her hand and turned away from the spoon.

"Okay," he said with a sigh. "At least you tried. Now let's get some questions answered, Miss Haydn." He patted her hand and rested his fingers on her arm for a moment, longer than seemed appropriate for a police interview. Chief Maxwell pulled out his notebook, and the handsome gentleman who fed her applesauce moments ago morphed into an all-business police chief.

He's doing his job, Piper. I'm sure he's this caring to everyone.

Piper sighed and focused on his questions so she could finally see her mom.

Piper closed her eyes when Chief Maxwell left the room. Everything hurt—her head, her throat, and her heart. A tear slipped from her eye and slid down her cheek.

I can't believe Trefor did this to me—to Daniel. I trusted him.

Piper's mom burst through the door and ran to the side of the bed. Tears streamed down her face, and she kissed Piper's forehead.

Piper's father stood behind Sarah. Tears rolled down his pale cheeks.

"Come on, everyone. It's not a funeral," Piper whispered.

"It very well could have been, Piper. It could have been." Jack Haydn's voice quivered. He hurried to the other side of her bed and patted her bandaged hand.

"I'm so sorry, baby," Sarah said. She smoothed Piper's hair away from her face and rested her cheek on Piper's forehead.

Jack rubbed Piper's arm. He opened his mouth, then closed his lips and glanced away.

"I've made a decision," Piper whispered. She cleared her throat and grimaced at the pain. "I'm going to pack my things and become a nun." She grinned at her parent's wide-eyed expressions.

Jack Haydn frowned. "Not sure where you're going with this, Piper. We're not Catholic."

Piper sighed. "I seem to have horrible discretion in the men I trust. I figure becoming a nun will save me from myself."

"Oh, sweetheart," Sarah said. "You are a kind, sweet, trusting soul. What these men did to you isn't your fault."

A tear trickled down Piper's cheek at her mother's soothing words. She choked back the sobs trying to escape. "I'm gonna need therapy." Her voice croaked, and she grinned at her parents.

Jack nodded. "We all are after *this*—I do believe." He patted her hand. "What's the agenda, Mother?" he asked Sarah.

Sarah checked her watch and smiled. "The nurse said after the doctor does rounds, we'll have a better idea when she can go home. It may be several hours 'til we see him. I'll wait if you want to go to work."

Jack nodded. "I hate to leave, but we have a couple of pressing issues. Call me for anything. I'll leave word with the office to interrupt if needed." He kissed Piper's forehead. "I'm going to bubble-wrap you and lock you away when I get home tonight."

"Thank you, Daddy," Piper whispered. "I love you."

"I love you t . . ." Jack choked, and his face crumpled. Tears ran down his face.

"Oh, Daddy. I'm fine." Piper smiled and patted her father's hand.

He nodded and turned to the door. "Anything. I mean it. If you need anything, you call me."

Piper nodded, and Sarah kissed her husband goodbye, then sank into the chair next to Piper's bed. "Oh, Piper Grace. I aged twenty-five years last night." She sighed.

"I'm sorry, Mom."

"You don't apologize, Piper. You never apologize for what someone else did to you. I'm so thankful you'll recover and come home to me." She blinked and rested her hand on her heart. "I can't dwell on what might have happened."

Rosie tapped on the door and peeked her head around. "Can I come in?" she whispered.

Piper held out her arms, and Rosie hugged her gently. "Good grief, Piper Haydn." Rosie stared at her with a frown. "When you're ready to talk about this, we're having a session. I cannot believe . . ." She trailed off.

Piper pointed to the door. "Who's out there?"

Rosie smiled, held up her fingers, and tapped one for each person she named. "Let's see, Pastor, of course. He's kept us all calm while we waited. Ruby brought coffee for everyone. Dominique brought brownies, and she saved one for you. Your brothers tried to come in here before me, but I threatened them." Rosie giggled, and her hoop earrings clanked. "Becky brought new magazines for the waiting room from the bookstore. Lillie stopped in but left a while ago to open her store. Cassidy brought cotton yarn for you, Mrs. Haydn. She said dishcloth knitting is mindless, and she figured your mind is already distracted enough."

Sarah smiled. "I couldn't pay attention to an intricate pattern if I tried right now. Please thank her for me."

Rosie continued naming names. "Basically, half the town is out there praying for you and hoping you'll pull through."

Piper smiled. "Tell them all thank you for me."

Rosie nodded. "Of course, friend. Oh, Lisa's here too." She raised her shoulder and grimaced. "She's desperate to speak with you."

"Send her in. I want to know what she has to say." Piper shifted in the bed, and Sarah jumped to help her adjust her position.

Rosie saluted. "Yes, boss. I'll bring her in to face the firing squad after I update everyone that you will indeed live to see another day."

Piper rolled her eyes. "You're incorrigible, Roosevelt."

Rosie curtsied. "And you love me anyway, Miss Haydn."

Piper laughed and groaned at the pain in her throat.

Sarah fussed over Piper, adjusting pillows and straightening the covers until Lisa peeked around the door.

"Can I come in, Piper?" she whispered.

Piper waved her in, and Lisa walked to the side of the hospital bed. She stared out the window and whispered. "I'm so sorry."

Piper reached for her hand. "What happened? Why did you take the money?"

Lisa pulled her hand away and fiddled with a tissue between her fingers. "At first, I took small amounts when I didn't have quite enough to pay my bills." She bit her lip and put her head down. "You never noticed, so I took more." Tears rolled down her cheeks, and she stared out the window.

"Why didn't you ask for help?"

Lisa sighed and smiled a shaky smile. "I always need help since my husband left. I get so tired of asking for help and not having enough. My pride took a hit when he left, and the hits kept coming. He's months behind in child support, and my second mortgage came due."

She glanced at Piper for the first time since entering the room. Tears rolled from her red-rimmed swollen eyes. "My credit isn't strong enough to refinance, so I took the money and paid the mortgage off. I planned to pay every penny back before you needed it for the scholarships." She bit her lip, and a sob escaped. "I can't. I don't know how I will pay you back."

Piper squeezed Lisa's hand. "I wish you'd come to me, Lisa. We would have figured out a way to help you. I'm sad I didn't know you were struggling."

Lisa's voice cracked. "My stupid pride kept me from telling anyone." She glanced at Piper and smoothed the blanket in front of her.

"Why did you disappear after the murder?" Piper shifted in the bed and reached for the water. Sarah helped her sip and fluffed her pillows.

Lisa dabbed her tears. "I knew with the police around, someone would discover the missing money. I didn't want to face blame for murder too."

"All that did was cause us to suspect you, Lisa. What about that night at your house when you told me I shouldn't be there? What was going on?" Piper asked.

Lisa frowned. "You surprised me for one thing. I stopped to feed the animals, and you came out of the darkness. I didn't know what you knew, and I panicked."

"Where did you go? Where were you hiding?" Piper frowned.

Lisa picked at the blanket covering Piper and glanced out the window. She bit her lip.

"Lisa?"

"At Trefor's," Lisa whispered and dropped her chin to her chest.

Piper's mouth fell open. "Did you know? Lisa. Did you know?"

Tears fell down Lisa's face, and her shoulders heaved. "No," she said, and her chin trembled. "I had no idea, Piper. I promise."

Sarah gasped. "You and your children hid with a murderer?"

"She didn't know, Mom." Piper patted her mother's hand.

"No. I absolutely did not know, and I'm so sorry. What kind of mother am I? What kind of human?"

"Lisa, you didn't know. I'll help you figure this out when I'm better."

"Thank you, Piper." Lisa nodded and wiped her eyes. She slipped from the room.

"What a mess, Mom," Piper whispered.

Sarah patted her arm. "Why don't you rest 'til the doctor comes in?"

"Sounds like a plan." Piper sighed and closed her eyes, drifting off to sleep once more.

Piper sank into bed in her childhood room. Her mom adjusted the covers and kissed her forehead. "Thanks, Mom." Piper sighed. "I'm so tired."

"Well, you sleep, sweetheart, and call if you need anything." Sarah pointed to Piper's phone on the bedside table. "I'll keep my ringer on so I can hear if you do." Sarah stood in the doorway and blew a kiss.

Piper smiled and closed her eyes. She dreamt of piano recitals, green porcelain frogs, tumbles downstairs, and a handsome man wearing a button-down shirt and blue jeans. She woke with a start and glanced around the dark room.

No monsters in the closet, I hope.

Piper groaned, grappling with the truth about Trefor and the picture of what she knew of him. Sure, he was a quirky guy with strange habits and tastes, but a murderer?

I'll never trust my perceptions again. How did I miss this?

A tear rolled down her cheek. Her head hurt, and her throat was still raw, but the idea that Trefor had killed Daniel because of her broke her heart. His *I did this for you* kept ringing in her mind. She sighed and attempted to sit up, but the pain in her head pushed her back onto the pillows.

The door opened, and her dad peeked in. "Are you awake, sweetheart?"

"Come in, Dad."

Jack Haydn flipped on her light. "Chief Maxwell is with me. Can he come in too?"

Piper nodded.

Jack stepped to the side of the bed and held Piper's hand. "How are you feeling? What can I get for you?"

"I'm just fine, Dad."

Chief Maxwell cleared his throat. "Miss Haydn, I trust you're feeling a little better tonight. We've finished interviewing Mr. Vaughn, and I have a couple of questions for you."

Piper nodded.

"First, when did you meet Trefor?"

Piper frowned and searched her memories. "A year ago? Something like that," she said.

The chief nodded. "And how did you come to be friends with him?"

Piper rubbed her forehead. "I don't know. We both teach music, and I went into the music store often enough that we became friends."

"And were you aware that Trefor fenced drugs for Daniel Graves?" Chief Maxwell asked.

Piper frowned. "What? I didn't know Daniel sold drugs. I didn't know Trefor sold drugs." She closed her eyes and rubbed her forehead. "I didn't know any of this. I wouldn't have had anything to do with Daniel or Trefor if I knew that. What's going to happen to Chase?"

The chief scribbled in his notebook and glanced at Piper. "Your brother cooperated with us and filled in a lot of details. He will face charges, but I'm hoping he gets a good plea deal for helping with the case. We've learned that Daniel and Trefor had an arrangement that went wrong. Trefor used his access to Notes Music Centre's warehouse to store and move drugs. Daniel came to confront Trefor one night, and Trefor killed him with . . ."

"A piano wire," Piper interrupted. "And the odd substance you found in Daniel's wound was aloe and methanol from the hand sanitizer Trefor used."

Chief Maxwell nodded. "Yes—how did you figure that out?"

"He always uses that hand sanitizer, and it's strong, so Rosie asked him where he got it once. He said Mexico because it's banned here. Then that cut on his hand. He claimed it was a paper cut, but the wound didn't seem to heal as a paper cut would. I put two and two together that night he came over. But why did he stuff Daniel into my Steinway?" She shuddered.

"He stored Daniel in your piano because he said, and I quote, 'Miss High and Mighty turned me down one too many times.'"

Piper sighed and picked at her blanket. "I don't know what to say."

"It seems he wanted to punish you, and he hoped we'd suspect you. He wanted to ruin your business because you hurt him. But I don't want you to think about that for another moment. He's responsible for his actions, and he had a problem with his drug dealer. The murder wasn't about you, although information leads us to believe they targeted you."

Piper's eyes widened, and she gasped. "What? Why me?"

"Your family's wealth and influence in Cranberry Harbor. Daniel's engagement to you and Trefor's supposed friendship with you led people to trust them. We aren't sure if they had other plans before they quarreled, but let's be thankful that they no longer have access to you." He snapped his notebook shut and left the room.

"Oh, Chief Maxwell?" Piper croaked, her throat still raw.

He stepped back into her room. "Yes, Miss Haydn?"

"Who found me that night? Why didn't Trefor kill me?"

The chief's cheeks flushed. He turned away and cleared his throat.

Jack Haydn interrupted. "It seems that Chief Maxwell personally patrolled your neighborhood, Piper. He didn't trust anyone but himself to watch over you, and he worked off the clock every night watching your house and neighborhood. I'm going to recommend him for a commendation."

"Thank you," Piper said. "But I don't know how you knew to come in or how Trefor didn't have a chance to finish me off."

"Well," Officer Maxwell said. "I knew he was in your home, but at the time, we hadn't suspected him, so I wasn't alarmed. But when I circled back around the neighborhood, I saw both of you on the stairs, and something looked off. When I parked and headed for your door, you fell back on him and tumbled down the stairs. I called backup and ran in."

"You were unconscious." Jack interrupted. "Trefor stood and reached for you, and the chief tackled him—hurt his shoulder in the process."

Chief Maxwell shrugged. "I'm fine. Glad I was there."

"Well, you were there on purpose, and you saved my daughter. Thank you." Jack's voice quivered, and he wiped his eyes.

"I can't thank you enough, sir," Piper said.

"Doing my job, Miss Haydn. I'm glad you're safe." He nodded. "I need to get back to the station, but I'll keep in touch." He waved at Jack and disappeared.

Piper blew out a sigh. "My goodness, Dad."

"I know," he said. "It's a lot to take in, but the good news is that he can't hurt you ever again. You're safe. Why don't you consider moving back home? Please?"

"I know you want to keep me safe, Daddy, but I'm almost thirty years old. I can't live at home forever. Besides, I love my old falling-apart house." She reached for her father's hand and squeezed.

"Well, I'm installing better security today, and you really should get a window shade for that huge window. You can see everything going on inside from the street," Jack said.

Piper laughed. "Well, that was a good thing the other night, Dad."

Jack leaned down and kissed Piper's forehead. "I love you, Piper Grace. Don't ever scare me like that again."

"I promise, Dad. I'll try very hard not to."

"Good girl," he whispered and squeezed her hand. "I'm going to let you rest."

Piper nodded and closed her eyes, thankful for a quiet room and a chance to clear her mind.

This time, she drifted to sleep thinking of Cranberry Harbor and a blushing police officer with kind eyes and a gentle smile.

Coda Two Weeks Later

Piper hurried toward the music academy carrying a large mug of coffee from Ruby's. The sounds of small-town USA preparing to celebrate the Fourth of July echoed around the parking lot. A tractor pulling a wagon idled near the front door. The farmer perched inside the cab leaned out and waved. Piper waved back and smiled. Several of Piper's staff wrapped red, white, and blue streamers around the trailer and hung a large American flag on the side. "Looks good!" Piper called.

Inside the academy, children practiced their dance moves and music. The youngest dancers would ride on the trailer with the youth symphony. The rest of the groups would walk behind, taking turns showing off dance moves or singing a patriotic song. Her oldest students would carry a banner advertising Haydn Music Academy.

Cranberry Harbor loved celebrations, but the Fourth of July was the town's specialty. Flags hung from every business and home, and red, white, and blue bunting appeared on every porch rail. Downtown businesses decorated their windows in patriotic themes to honor veterans and thank heroes. The restaurants and cafes sold red, white, and blue sweets. Dominque sold her annual cream puffs packed full of red, white, or blue cream and patriotic sprinkles at Sweetberry's. Ruby sold cherry-, blueberry-, or cream-flavored iced coffees to hungry parade-goers. After the parade, families would scatter and celebrate with cookouts, picnics, and a splash in Glacier Lake. At night people from Cranberry Harbor and the local communities would spread blankets on the grass in the park to watch the fireworks sponsored by Haydn Orchards.

Piper planned to enjoy all the festivities and looked forward to cooling off with a huge bomb pop from her mother's freezer this afternoon. But right now she needed to gather herself before the busy day rolled into action.

She grabbed the handle of the auditorium door and jerked it open before her fear took over. Piper sank into a seat in the back row of the dark auditorium. The light above the stage shone on her old grand piano. The owner of Notes Music Centre promised a new piano, but Piper had to wait another year while Steinway built the instrument.

After much discussion, Piper and her teachers had canceled the end-of-the-school-year recital—too much trauma. She thanked her students for their dedication and promised they would have an opportunity to share their talents at the Christmas recital. Hopefully, the work Piper did in her counselor's office would kick in and help her face hosting a recital. She blew out a breath in the quiet room and ran through the events of the past several weeks.

Chase faced charges for his part in the drug scheme. The Haydn family had faced the fallout of his wayward activities before, but Jack insisted on counseling and rehab for Chase this time. "No more," he had said.

Trefor sat in jail awaiting trial—another thing Piper's counseling would prepare her to face.

Piper decided she wouldn't press charges against Lisa, but they met with Lenny to sign an agreement. Lisa would repay the scholarship money but wouldn't handle the academy's finances.

Piper played with the hem of the patriotic fireworks scarf and remembered all the support during the past days. Dominique stopped at her house several times a week with a chocolate treat. Maisy kept her supplied with relaxing and healing teas. Lillie brought her a floral print scarf, and Becky showed up on her porch with a pile of books. "And a journal," she said, "to write down your feelings so you can heal."

Pastor and Mrs. James met with her at the Haydn home one afternoon and clarified her question.

"No," Pastor James said. "You aren't guilty of cheating with Daniel Graves. He bore the guilt."

Piper's heart lifted after their visit. She had known she wasn't guilty, but her mind accused her often enough to leave her head spinning and her heart sad.

Chief Maxwell checked on her one time, assuring her that Trefor wouldn't hurt her. His kind eyes searched hers for a moment when he asked, "Are you okay? Truly okay?" Piper had nodded, and he said, "Good." She hadn't seen him since, but she would attend his commendation ceremony. Jack Haydn had pulled many strings in Madison to get the ball rolling, and Piper appreciated her father's efforts. Chief Maxwell deserved all the praise for saving her life.

Piper's teachers kept the academy running in her absence. They covered her lessons, cleaned and organized her office, and fielded calls from parents. Piper breathed a prayer of thanks for each one.

Her parents hovered and spoiled her with attention. Piper had decided to stay at the Haydn home while she healed. Her parents needed time to deal with all the stress of the past days. "But I'm going home after the Fourth of July, Dad," she had said. Tomorrow she would step out of the cocoon she had hidden in over the past weeks and reclaim her life.

"Trefor doesn't win. Daniel doesn't win. My fear doesn't win," she whispered in the empty auditorium. Piper had much to look forward to—a new niece or nephew soon, a thriving music academy. She had friends who adored her and a family who loved her. Piper stood and glanced around the auditorium and smiled. "Life is good," she whispered. "I'm good."

The door burst open, and the sound of trumpets and drums from a marching band drifted in. "Piper!" Rosie yelled. "Come quick! I have something to show you!" She grabbed Piper's hand and pulled her to the parking lot.

The sound of the marching band grew louder, and Piper glanced around the parking lot at the commotion. Little dancers climbed over the side of the trailer to find their spots, and older dancers lined up behind teachers and banners. The town fire trucks lined the street in front of the academy, their red lights flashing.

A warm breeze blew, and Piper tucked a strand of hair behind her ears. "Hurry up, Rosie—the parade will start soon, and we're driving the Escalade."

Rosie dragged Piper to the corner of the parking lot and pointed. Piper stared at the beat-up Volkswagen van. Faded yellow paint chipped and peeled, and the bald tires gave the van a tilt. A large crack ran down the windshield, and the side door hung crooked.

Piper's eyes widened. "Oh, my, Rosie— what in the world?"

Rosie smiled and nodded her head. "Isn't it amazing? Look at this." She pulled the door open, and Piper turned her head away when the scent of musty carpet and long-forgotten fast-food spills assaulted her nose.

"What exactly am I looking at here, Roosevelt?" Piper frowned at her friend.

"Fabulous, right?" Rosie clapped her hands, and her bracelets jingled a cheery sound. "Remember I said I had something to show you? Here she is, Piper. Meet Bess."

Piper tilted her head to the side and squinted. Nope. It still looked—and smelled—awful. "Where did you get her? You should ask for your money back." Piper grimaced and covered her nose.

Rosie unrolled a canvas awning, and a piece of moldy fabric dropped onto Piper's foot. Piper grimaced and jiggled her foot until the dank material fell off her sandal.

"I found her on marketplace and ran to Appleton with Truman the other day. She's perfect, isn't she?" Rosie's eyes sparkled.

Piper raised her eyebrows and choked back a laugh. "*Perfect* isn't the word I'd use. What are you planning to do with this thing?"

"I'm going to restore Bess and use her for my glamper." Rosie smiled and danced a little jig, the sequins on her shirt collar spreading red, white, and blue rainbows across the asphalt.

"*Glamper?*" Piper said.

"Glamour, camper, glamper," Rosie said. "When she's ready to roll, you and I are going glamping."

"Oh, no, no, no, no, no, Roosevelt Hale. Piper Haydn does not camp." Piper waggled her finger at Rosie.

"This is different—glamorous camping. Aren't you listening?" Rosie shut the side door and smiled at Piper.

"Glamorous camping is a night at the Ritz, Rosie. I will never, ever set foot in that thing, much less sleep in it. I don't care how glamorous—not happening." Piper stomped her foot and shook her head.

The tractor full of students pulled out of the driveway, followed by groups of dancers. Piper smiled and hurried to the Escalade. "Come on, Rosie! We have a parade to catch!" she called.

Rosie hopped in the passenger seat and donned her Uncle Sam top hat. She rolled down the window and yelled, "God bless the USA!"

Piper laughed at her zany friend, pulled out of the parking lot behind her students, and followed as the parade rolled into action. "I love you, Roosevelt Hale, but I promise you that I will never 'glamp' with you."

Rosie waved out the window and yelled, "Happy Fourth of July!" She turned to Piper and said, "We'll see, Piper. We'll see."

Piper rolled her eyes and followed the parade route, waving at the onlookers and smiling at the sea of red, white, and blue. "Thank you, God, for Cranberry Harbor, USA," she whispered and smiled.

Peace flooded her heart, and the fear she had carried lifted for the first time in weeks. Life would return to normal, and Piper would regain her happiness.

Life is good. She smiled. *But I will never go 'glamping' with Rosie.*

A thank you—

*To Chief Aaron Chapin for indulging his aunt and answering police procedural questions.

   *To Michael Lyon for finding a brand of fancy pen that Piper's father might use.

   *To my siblings, Rebekah Kotlar, Rachel Hershberger, and John Bonner, for once again helping me brainstorm and giving me the best ideas. I love you.

   *To my friend J. Dahlke RN, BSN, CNI, for helping me understand how nurses might talk to a patient waking up from trauma.

   *To my friend Vicky O. for helping me figure out the chemical components that may show up in an investigation.

*To Ross Martin, our music pastor, for letting me know that a Steinway crate is indeed big enough to hold a body.

*To Patricia McCann London, my sensitivity editor—to make sure I wrote respectfully and accurately when I included African American characters in my story.

*To my alpha team— Kathy Ann, Tonya Young, Miranda Pautz, Crystal Thornton, Laurie Herlich, Laurie Griepentrog, Christina Lyon, Rebekah Kotlar, Christy Reeder, Marsha Landro, Karla Bolender, Jackie Koll, Rachel Hershberger, Xanthe Vanderputt, Ashley Hawley, John Bonner. Thank you for making me work hard to write a great story. I appreciate all your help, encouragement, and mistake-finding.

*To you, my readers. Thank you for giving my novel a chance. I appreciate you. Please leave a review of Murder Goes Solo where you bought your copy. Thank you.

Murder Goes Solo Playlist

Beethoven: Rage Over A Lost Penny
Berlioz: Symphonie fantastique, Op. 14: 1. Reveries-Passions

Chopin: Preludes, Op. 28: No. 15, Sostenuto in D-Flat Major
"Raindrops"

Debussy: Claire de Lune
Debussy: La Mer, L. 109: I. De l'aube a midi sur la mer
Debussy: Mandoline
Debussy: La Fille aux Cheveux de Lin, L. 33
Debussy: Reverie, CD 76, L. 68
Debussy: Petite suite, L. 65: En bateau
Debussy: Douze Etudes: X. Etude pour les sonorites opposees
Dino: Amazing Grace
Dino: To God Be the Glory

Rimsky-Korsakov: Flight of the Bumblebee

Tangled Lines: Grandma's Tea

Vivaldi: 4 Seasons, Summer 3-Presto

I compiled this playlist on Spotify. If you'd like to find it, search for *Piper Haydn Murder Goes Solo Malissa Chapin*

To thank you for purchasing my book, email me a photo or screenshot of your purchase receipt for Murder Goes Solo, and I'll email you a set of custom-created Piper Haydn paper dolls. Free—to say thank you!

If you borrowed Murder Goes Solo from a library, visit my website www.malissachapin.com and sign up for my email list. Then email me that you did so, and I'll email you the free set of Piper paper dolls to thank you for reading my book!

Malissa Chapin grew up reading books, making up stories, and vowing to publish a book before turning twelve. She's a few years late for her goal but still devours books and makes up stories.

Malissa loves creating with words, yarn, fabric, and watercolors. She enjoys sharing her faith, reading, collecting vintage treasures, drinking coffee, playing the piano, homeschooling her bonus baby, and looking on the bright side. She lives and sometimes freezes in Wisconsin with her family and a crazy cat.

the
ROAD
HOME

MALISSA
CHAPIN

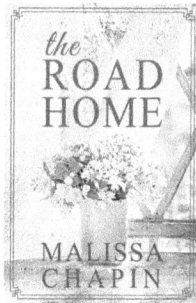

Sometimes your past catches up with you. Sometimes you confront your past.

When a life of tragedy leaves Audra March with a desperate desire for acceptance, she blurs the line between right and wrong. She runs from her tainted past and creates a new identity in a small Wisconsin town.
When she discovers a vintage recipe box, her search for the owner takes Audra across the country and sets her on a collision course with the truth. With the help of an Appalachian preacher and the long-buried deception of an elderly woman, Audra learns the value of honesty and trust. For the first time, she finds hope for her future.

But when her carefully crafted identity is at risk, her resolve is tested. Will she run again? Or will she confront the consequences of her past? Can the truth set her free?

HOPE FOR CHRISTMAS

MALISSA CHAPIN
A Christmas Novella

Merry Noel is a busy woman with no time or patience to celebrate holidays. But when she's fired after going berserk at the office Christmas party, she goes back to Wisconsin to visit her mom for the first time in years.

A wise man named Joe, a blizzard, and an unexpected guest help Merry recapture her joy and bring her Hope for Christmas.

www.ingramcontent.com/pod-product-compliance
Lightning Source LLC
Chambersburg PA
CBHW062131020426
42335CB00013B/1174